# *Advanced International English*

## Nick Brieger and Andy Jackson

Cassell

Cassell Publishers Limited
Artillery House
Artillery Row
London SW1P 1RT

First published 1989
Reprinted 1989

The Authors and Publishers would like to thank the following for permission to use their copyright photographs:

Topham Picture Library, p 16; Carlos Reyes, Andes Picture Library, p 19; Hubertus Kanus, Barnaby's Picture Library, p 20; Kobal Collection, p 27; Sally and Richard Greenhill, p 31, p 39, p 42 (right), p 59, p 81 and p 132, Barnaby's Picture Library, p 31 and HK Maitland, p 32, Jill Chamberlain, p 39, J Harrigan p 41 and Tony Boxall, p 153 of Barnabys; Camilla Jessel, p 35; S and G Press, p 41; Douglas Dickens, p 49, p 97, and p 156; BTA p 46, p 53, and p 95; Christine Osborne, Middle East pictures and publicity, p 56; David W Jones, p 60, A.F. Kersting, p 63; Will Green, p 67; Scottish Tourist Board, p 67; Finnish Tourist Board, p 70; J. Allen Cash, p 77, p 84, p 91, p 119, p 125, p 133, p 139 and p 150; BBC Hulton Picture Library, p 100; BBC Ceefax, p 114; Thomas Cook, p 115; Brian and Sal Shuel, p 118 and p 142; Science Photo Library, p 122; Guildhall Library, p 128; Universal Pictorial Press, p 143 and p 146; Jan Kopec, Camera Press, p 147.

We are grateful too, to the following for their help with the recorded material: Roland Hindmarsh; Sidney Rudgeon; Giovanni Leonetti; Rhona Jackson; Helen Stansfield; Peter Davies; John James; Rev. James Boyd; Sayid Khalid; Leslie Philips; Arthur Fisk; David Barnes; Eric Morton; Jane Wallis; Mike Bishop; Ann Corsellis; Rosa Gran; Charlie Dwight; Mike Stevens; James Tollinton; Jo Whitehead; Nigel Barker; Tomoko Yoshida; John Wakely; Eileen Phipp; Arthur Flagstaff; Gabriel Ndong; Jean Martenne; John Barnes; Frank Hobson; Ana Maria Zatarain; Andy Johnson; George Challoner; Helen Stopoulos; Bill Grant; Mary Marsden; June McDonald; Erik Jonsson; George Roberts

British Library Cataloguing in Publication Data

Brieger, Nick, *1948*–
    Advanced international English.
    1. English language — For non-English
    speaking students
    I. Title   II. Jackson, Andy, *1943*–
    428.2'4
    ISBN 0–304–31289–4

*Design by Carlton Larodé*
*Illustrations by Steven Garner, Gerald Wood, Carlton Larodé*
*and Ian Foulis & Associates*
*Typesetting by Graphicraft typesetters Ltd.*
*Printed in Great Britain by The Bath Press, Bath, Avon*

# ACKNOWLEDGEMENTS

The Authors and Publishers are grateful for permission to reproduce copyright material from the following sources:

*How to be an Alien* (1946) by George Mikes, published by André Deutsch Ltd; 'American and British English' and 'English Names' from *Our Language* (1950) by Simeon Potter, reproduced by permission of Penguin Books Ltd; 'Anatomy of Burglary' by Leslie Watkins and Lois Fletcher, reprinted with permission from *Reader's Digest*, © 1985 The Reader's Digest; 'Autobiography of an Urban Marginal' by Juan Ruisque-Alcairio and Ray Bromley, from *Work and Poverty in Third World Cities* by Ray Bromley and Chris Gerry, reprinted by permission of John Wiley & Sons Ltd; 'A Crisis in Education' by Margaret Jay, from *The Listener*, 20 April 1986; 'Qur'anic Schools' by Abdulaziz El Khoussy, from *UNESCO Courier*, August 1983; 'The Christian Churches in Britain' from *Britain 1986 Handbook*, Crown Copyright 1986, reprinted with permission of the Controller, HMSO; 'A Village Called Nanpur' by P Mohanti, from *UNESCO Courier*, June 1983; 'The Lake District', reproduced from *One's Man England* by W G Hoskins with the permission of BBC Enterprises Ltd; 'Turkey for the Tourist', extracted from 'Asia for Beginners' by Brian Sewell, *Sunday Times Magazine*, 14 December 1986; 'How to Tell if Someone is Lying', copyright Alan Pease 1981, from *Body Language: How to Read Others' Thoughts by Their Gestures* published by Camel Publishing Company, PO Box 350 Avalon Beach, NSW 2107, Australia; 'Women and Multinationals' from *Women and Multinationals from World View*, edited by P Ayrton and T Engelhardt, published by Pluto Press; 'City of a Thousand Minarets' by John Feeny, reprinted with permission from *Reader's Digest*, © 1984 The Reader's Digest; 'Food' from *Class* by Jilly Cooper, published by Methuen London; 'Why Africa Goes Hungry' by Brian Leith, Television Producer with BBC Natural History Unit at Bristol; 'Viewdata and Teletext', from *Discovering Communications* (1983) by J Stanstell, published by Longman Group UK Ltd, 'Rolling Back the Waves', reprinted with permission from *The Economist*, 12–18 April 1986; 'Mayhew's London' by J Champkin from *New Internationalist*, February 1986; 'A Life in the Day of Peter Walker' by Bill Kellon, *Sunday Times Magazine*, 15 December 1986; 'Bishop Tutu', extracted from 'Tutu on a Tightrope' by Peter Godwin, *Sunday Times Magazine*, 8 June 1986; 'How to Take Your Time' by Lowell Ponte, reprinted with permission from *Reader's Digest*, © 1983 The Reader's Digest; 'A New Sight in the Sky' (extract) by Oliver Gillie, *Sunday Times Magazine*, 25 May 1986.

While every attempt has been made to trace copyright owners, the Publishers would be pleased to hear from any other parties who feel they hold rights to any of the material that has been included.

# CONTENTS

The modules are designed so that A and C units are based on UK themes, and B and D units are based on broader themes. In each module, the A and B units are reading-based, while the C and D units are listening-based. For the B and D units, where the theme focuses on a particular part of the world not obvious from the title, this is indicated below.

# CONTENTS

# PHONETIC SYMBOLS

## VOWELS

| SYMBOL | KEY WORD |
|--------|----------|
| æ | sad |
| ɑ: | farm |
| e | red |
| ɪ | pin |
| i: | feel |
| o | hot |
| ɔ: | caught |
| u | put |
| u: | shoot |
| ʌ | cut |
| ə | about |
| ə: | bird |
| aɪ | nice |
| au | now |
| eɪ | take |
| eə | hair |
| ɪə | near |
| ɔɪ | boy |
| uə | sure |
| əu | pole |
| aɪə | fire |
| auə | flower |
| eɪə | player |
| ɔɪə | employer |
| əuə | blower |

## CONSONANTS

| SYMBOL | KEY WORD |
|--------|----------|
| b | bad |
| d | dog |
| ð | this |
| dʒ | jar |
| f | far |
| g | go |
| h | help |
| j | yellow |
| k | cat |
| l | leg |
| m | mother |
| n | now |
| ŋ | sing |
| p | pig |
| r | rose |
| s | say |
| ʃ | ship |
| t | time |
| tʃ | chop |
| θ | thing |
| v | voice |
| w | wet |
| z | zebra |
| ʒ | leisure |

### STRESS
The stressed syllable in each word or phrase is marked by /ˈ/ before the syllable. The above is a slightly simplified version of the phonetic symbol notation used in most standard learners' dictionaries.

# PARTS OF SPEECH

Before each reading text, a vocabulary list is given, indicating the part of speech and giving the meaning of the word in its specific context, with a definition of the type used in advanced learners' dictionaries. Below are the abbreviations used for the parts of speech:

| | |
|---|---|
| *abbrev* | abbreviation |
| *adj* | adjective |
| *adv* | adverb |
| *adv phr* | adverbial phrase |
| *n* | noun |
| *n phr* | noun phrase |
| *n pl* | plural noun |
| *prep phr* | prepositional phrase |
| *vi* | intransitive verb |
| *vt* | transitive verb |
| *v phr* | phrasal verb/verb phrase |

# INTRODUCTION

*Advanced International English* is a language course for advanced adult students who wish to apply and improve their language skills around a wide range of topic areas dealing with world issues. The broad scope of the book should make it of interest to specialist and non-specialist students of English of all nationalities who wish to extend their experience and knowledge, both of English and through the medium of English. More specifically the materials develop the skills of listening, speaking, reading, writing, vocabulary and pronunciation, as well as review, extend, and practise selected patterns of the language. The book can be used as:
— classroom materials
— self-study materials
— classroom + self-study materials (see 'Roles of Teacher and Student' below)
The criteria used in the selection of materials have been interest, variety, and authenticity — with the aim of providing stimulating practice for integrated skill development.

*Advanced International English* is aimed at students who are either preparing for, or have taken, the Cambridge 'Certificate of Proficiency in English', or are at an equivalent level. Although not intended as an examination preparation course, it naturally develops language skills required in advanced level examinations.

*Advanced International English* has been designed so that it can be used on extensive or intensive courses. Its flexible organisation enables teachers to develop study programmes for different purposes and for different course durations. The materials are designed around:
— input texts (listening and reading)
— focus activities (language patterns, vocabulary and pronunciation)
— output tasks (speaking and writing)
The input texts provide platforms in terms of both their informational content and their linguistic content. The focus activities highlight the linguistic content; the output tasks the informational content. In this way texts constitute the basis for both informational and linguistic activities.

In informational terms the materials develop listening and reading skills (via output tasks) in the areas of:
— extracting gist information
— extracting detailed information
— structuring information
— inferring meaning from context
In linguistic terms the materials provide:
— presentation and practice of language patterns
— presentation and practice of vocabulary and idiom
— pronunciation practice activities
— familiarisation with different accents (British and foreign), registers and styles of English
In informational/linguistic terms the materials develop speaking and writing skills around;
— discussion
— debate
— free writing activities
Finally, we hope that the materials will help to broaden the students' experience and knowledge through the medium of English.

## I   Setting the scene

## 2   Vocabulary

| | | |
|---|---|---|
| tolerable *adj* | (l.3) | quite good, not too bad |
| convince *vt* | (l.4) | make (someone) believe or be sure |
| impression *n* | (l.16) | idea, feeling given to another person |
| mutter *vi* | (l.18) | speak unclearly in a low voice |
| air *n* | (l.29) | appearance, feeling |
| interminably *adv* | (l.36) | endlessly, extremely |
| bully *vt* | (l.41) | use your strength or power to hurt weaker people |
| allegiance *n* | (l.44) | support, loyalty |
| obedience *n* | (l.45) | doing what you are told to do |
| abominable *adj* | (l.56) | hateful, causing great dislike |

## 3   Text

While you are reading the text, answer the following questions:
a)   How long did it take the writer to realise that he would never speak English perfectly?
b)   What, according to the writer, is the most important adjective you need in England?
c)   Which skill do foreigners develop most accurately?

# ■ HOW TO BE AN ALIEN

When I arrived in England I thought I knew English. After I'd been here an hour I realized that I did not understand one word. In the first week I picked up a tolerable working knowledge of the language and the next seven years convinced me gradually but thoroughly that I would never know it really well, let alone perfectly.

Remember that those five hundred words an average Englishman uses are far from being the whole vocabulary of the language. You may learn five thousand and yet another fifty thousand and still you may come across another fifty thousand you have never heard of before, and nobody else either.

If you reside here long enough you will find out to your greatest amazement that the adjective 'nice' is not the only adjective the language possesses, in spite of the fact that in the first three years you do not need to learn to use any other adjectives. You can say that the weather is nice, Mr So-and-so is nice, Mrs So-and-so's clothes are nice, you had a nice time, and all this will be very nice.

Then there is the problem of accent. The easiest way of giving the impression of having a good accent or no foreign accent at all is to hold an unlit pipe in your mouth, to mutter between your teeth and terminate all your sentences with the question: 'isn't it?'. People will not understand much, but they are accustomed to that and they will get an excellent impression.

I have known quite a number of foreigners who tried hard to acquire an Oxford accent. The advantage of this is that you give the idea of being permanently in the company of Oxford dons and lecturers on medieval numismatics; the disadvantage is that the permanent singing is rather a strain on your throat and that it is a type of affectation that even many English people find it hard to keep up incessantly. You may fall out of it, speak naturally, and then where are you?

The Mayfair accent can be highly recommended too. The advantages of Mayfair English are that it unites the affected air of the Oxford accent with the uncultured flavour of a half-educated professional hotel-dancer. But rather more successful attempts to put on a highly cultured air have been made on the polysyllabic lines. Many foreigners who have learnt Latin and Greek in school discover with amazement and satisfaction that the English language has absorbed a huge amount of ancient Latin and Greek expressions, and they realize that (a) it is much easier to learn these expressions than the much simpler English words; (b) that these words as a rule are interminably long and make a simply superb impression when talking to the greengrocer, the porter and the insurance agent.

Imagine, for instance, that the porter of the block of flats where you live remarks sharply that you must not put your dustbin out in front of your door before 7.30am. Should you answer 'Please don't bully me,' a loud and tiresome argument may follow, and certainly the porter will be proved right, because you are sure to find a clause in your contract (small print, bottom of the last page) that the porter is always right and you owe absolute allegiance and unconditional obedience to him. Should you answer, however, with these words: 'I repudiate your petulant expostulations', the argument will be closed at once, the porter will be proud of having such a highly cultured man in the block, and from that day onwards you may, if you please, get up at four o'clock in the morning and hang your dustbin out of the window.

When you know all the long words it is advisable to start learning some of the short ones, too.

Finally, there are two important points to bear in mind:

1. Do not forget that it is much easier to write English than to speak English, because you can write without a foreign accent.

2. In a bus and in other public places it is more advisable to speak softly in good German than to shout in abominable English.

Anyway, this whole language business is not at all easy. After spending eight years in this country, the other day I was told by a very kindly lady: 'But why do you complain? You really speak a most excellent accent without the slightest English.'

*(From **How to Be an Alien** by George Mikes)*

2

# 4  Language study

## a)  Vocabulary

George Mikes points out that English often has parallel expressions, one from Latin or Greek, and the other from Anglo-Saxon origins. The former usually sound more formal and 'educated', while the latter are more common in everyday use. Here are some of the expressions used in the passage. Pair them with their more formal/informal equivalent:

| | | | |
|---|---|---|---|
| 1 | pick up | a) | possess |
| 2 | find out | b) | terminate |
| 3 | keep up | c) | accustomed to |
| 4 | have | d) | accumulate |
| 5 | used to | e) | reside |
| 6 | always | f) | ancient |
| 7 | live | g) | discover |
| 8 | end | h) | permanently |
| 9 | old | i) | maintain |

## b)  Useful words and phrases

i)    let alone     (l.5)
ii)   far from      (l.7)
iii)  as a rule     (l.36)
iv)   bear in mind  (l.52)

Rewrite the following sentences using one of the above expressions:

1  They are not at all happy about this.
2  I hope you will remember what I've just said.
3  She generally prefers tea to coffee in the evenings.
4  There is not enough food for four people and certainly not six.

## c)  Language focus: intensifiers with comparison of adjectives

The text uses some expressions of comparison, such as: 'rather more successful', 'much easier', 'much simpler'.

The following table gives you a list of intensifiers in ascending order that can be used with a comparative adjective to modify the degree of comparison:

| |
|---|
| slightly |
| a little |
| a bit |
| |
| rather |
| somewhat |
| |
| much |
| a lot |
| a great deal |
| far |

## d)  Activity

Write sentences comparing the two items given, using the adjective associated with the noun supplied, together with an appropriate intensifier from the above list: The first one has been done for you.

1  Mount Everest — K2 (height)
   Mount Everest is slightly higher than K2.

2  The Amazon — the Thames (length)

3  An armchair — a bicycle seat (comfort)

4   Riding a bike — flying a plane (ease)

_____

5   A rat — a mouse (size)

_____

6   A Mercedes — a Volkswagen (cost)

_____

7   Men — women (strength)

_____

8   The Sahara — the Arctic (temperature)

_____

9   The Mediterranean — the Atlantic (pollution)

_____

10   Charles Darwin — Captain Scott (fame)

_____

# 5   Transfer

**a)   Text**

Read through the text once more and decide whether, according to the author, the following statements are true or false:

1   The author had already learnt English before he came to Britain.
2   The average Englishman uses a range of about 5000 words.
3   The commonest adjective in English is 'nice'.
4   Pipe smokers have the best English accents.
5   The Oxford accent is the standard British accent.
6   Words of Latin or Greek origin are simpler than English words.
7   British people are impressed by long words.
8   Dustbins are normally collected before 7.30 in the morning in England.
9   It is easier to make yourself understood in English if you shout.
10   The author has a strong foreign accent.

**b)   Discussion**

Is it necessary to speak English with no foreign accent? Can anybody learn to do this or is it easier or more difficult depending on your native language?

# 6   Writing

**Write about one of these:**

a)   Anyone can learn a second language perfectly if they have the time and opportunity.
b)   Describe the ways in which English has influenced your language.

# MODULE I
## LANGUAGE B

## I  Setting the scene

## 2  Vocabulary

| | | |
|---|---|---|
| found *vt* | (l.4) | begin the development of something |
| seize *vt* | (l.5) | attack or take control of |
| ratify *vt* | (l.7) | make something official by signing |
| outbreak *n* | (l.11) | beginning |
| famine *n* | (l.13) | serious lack of food |
| drive *vt* | (l.13) | force or compel |
| absorption *n* | (l.22) | being taken in, becoming part of something |
| jeopardy *n* | (l.27) | danger |
| legacy *n* | (l.32) | something passed on or left behind after death |
| aver *vt* | (l.34) | accept or approve |
| sanction *vt* | (l.41) | state forcefully, declare |
| unduly *adv* | (l.45) | too much |

## 3  Text

While reading the text, find brief answers to the following questions:

a)  What date was the most important in American history from the point of view of language?

b)  Into how many periods of linguistic development does the writer divide the history of the USA?

c)  What prevented Webster from simplifying the spelling of American English?

# ■AMERICAN & BRITISH ENGLISH

The language taken by John Smith to Virginia in 1607 and by the Plymouth Fathers to Massachusetts in 1620 was the English of Spenser and Shakespeare. During the following century and a half most of the colonies that settled in New England were British, but the Dutch founded New Amsterdam and
5 held it until it was seized by the British in 1664 and re-named after the King's brother, the Duke of York. When, on 17th September 1787, the thirteen colonies on the Atlantic seaboard ratified the Federal Constitution, they comprised four million English-speaking people, most of whom still lived east of the Appalachian Mountains. From the linguistic point of view this was the first and decisive stage in
10 the history of American English.

During the period from 1787 to the outbreak of the Civil War in 1861 new states were created west of the Appalachians, and fresh immigrants came in large numbers from Ireland and Germany. The potato famine of 1845 drove one and a half million Irishmen to seek homes in the New World and the European revolution of 1848
15 drove as many Germans to settle in Pennsylvania and the Middle West.

The third period, from the end of the Civil War to the present day, was marked by the arrival of Scandinavians, Slavs, and Italians. In the closing decades of the nineteenth century one million Scandinavians, or one fifth of the whole population of Norway and Sweden, crossed the Atlantic Ocean, and settled, for the most part,
20 in Minnesota and the Upper Mississippi Valley. They were soon followed by millions of Eastern Europeans, and as the great North American Republic took shape with the attachment of French and Spanish populations and the absorption of Chinese and Japanese who landed on the Pacific coast, so the cosmopolitan character of the United States became more and more accentuated. Further, negroes from
25 Africa have come to number over twelve millions.

At no time, however, has the speech of Washington and Jefferson, of Jackson and Lincoln, stood in jeopardy. Never has there existed any real danger that English might not prove capable of completely assimilating these immigrant tongues. The literary language, indeed, has seldom diverged perceptibly from the old country. In
30 spelling, vocabulary, in pronunciation and the syntax of colloquial speech and slang, however, divergences persist. The distinctive features of American orthography are largely a legacy bequeathed by Noah Webster, whose American Spelling Book first appeared in 1783. The born reformer, he was determined to effect drastic changes: 'Common sense and convenience,' he averred, 'would lead me to write public,
35 favor, nabor, hed, proov, hiz, giv, det, ruf and wel instead of publick, favour, neighbour, head, prove, his, give, debt, rough and well'. But Webster wanted to make money and he sought a market for his book on both sides of the Atlantic. He was therefore advised by his publisher to modify his drastic changes considerably. Only the first two changes — public and favor — were allowed to remain. Today,
40 the third unabridged edition of Webster's New International Dictionary is the accepted authority in the American courts. It sanctions such spellings as '-or' for '-our', '-er' for '-re', one consonant for two in 'traveler', 'jewelry' and 'wagon', '-s-' for '-c-' in the nouns 'defense', 'offense' and 'practise', and various simplifications such as 'ax', 'catalog', 'check', 'jail' and 'program'.
45 On arriving in the United States, the Englishman is made unduly aware of differences in vocabulary because these figure rather prominently in the language of transport and travel. He finds himself checking his baggage, bags or grips instead of registering his luggage. This is placed in a freight elevator worked by an elevator operator who looks just like a lift attendant. Our English visitor is surprised to find
50 that subway is far more than a way under for pedestrians: it is the counterpart to the London underground. He goes to the 'information bureau' not the inquiry office, and is told to consult a 'schedule' rather than a timetable.

Finally, among the more outstanding features of American pronunciation a few may be noted here. In words like 'for', 'door', 'farm' and 'lord', the 'r' is still retained
55 as a fricative, whereas in Southern English it is silent except when it is naturally pronounced as a so-called 'linking 'r', in expressions like 'for ever', and 'the door opens'. Americans pronounce words like 'dance', 'fast', 'half', and 'path' with a low front sound (as in present-day Southern English 'cat'). They pronounce words like 'dock', 'fog' and 'hot' with a low back sound (as in present-day Southern English
60 'car' shortened), and 'beating' sounds very much (but not quite) like 'beading', 'matter' like 'madder' and 'metal' like 'medal'.

*(From **Our Language** by Simeon Potter)*

NEW YORK HILTON

ELEVATOR

EXCUSE ME, BUT WHERE'S THE LIFT?

6

# 4 Language study

### a) Vocabulary

Fill in the following table using words you have found in the text and others from your own knowledge.

| Noun (Concept/Action) | Noun (Agent) | Verb |
|---|---|---|
| immigration | | |
| | | publish |
| foundation | | |
| | informant | |
| | creator | |
| | | revolt |
| | originator | |
| reformation | | |
| | | edit |
| | | generate |

### b) Useful words and phrases: common collocations

Certain words are commonly associated with others in English to form common collocations. Here are some phrases from the text; pair them with the appropriate word from the second column.

| | | | |
|---|---|---|---|
| 1 | in _____ numbers | a) | drastic |
| 2 | the first and _____ stage | b) | prominently |
| 3 | for the _____ part | c) | outstanding |
| 4 | any _____ danger | d) | large |
| 5 | a legacy _____ by Webster | e) | most |
| 6 | to make _____ changes | f) | unduly |
| 7 | the _____ authority | g) | decisive |
| 8 | made _____ aware | h) | bequeathed |
| 9 | figure _____ in the language | i) | real |
| 10 | the _____ features | j) | accepted |

### c) Language focus: subject-verb inversion

In the fourth paragraph of the text, the first two sentences have the subject and verb inverted because of the adverb at the beginning. There is only a small group of words or phrases, placed at the beginning for emphasis, that cause this. The commonest are:

never
at no time
seldom
rarely
hardly (ever)
under no circumstances
so quickly/gently/suddenly/etc

They are normally used only in more formal kinds of English.

### d) Activity

Rewrite the following sentences by moving the underlined word or phrase to its more usual position and making any other changes necessary. The first one has been done for you.

1  Rarely have I seen such a beautiful sight.
   I have rarely seen such a beautiful sight.
   _____

2  Under no circumstances should you go there. (Careful!)
   _____

3  So rapidly did the pilot alter course that the passengers were thrown
   about violently.
   _____

4  Only yesterday did I realise my error.
   _____

5  Hardly had he begun his speech when the lights failed.
   _____

6  Seldom have I enjoyed a concert so much.
   _____

7  Never was the child allowed to play with others.
   _____

8  Hardly had we time to take cover before the heavens opened.
   _____

9  Only after being closely questioned did he admit his part in the affair.
   _____

10  Rarely have I had the opportunity to visit so many interesting places.
   _____

# 5  Transfer

## a)  Text

Using the text and your own experience, make a list of all the words or
expressions in British English that are different in American English (spelling or
whole word). Here are some to start you off:

| British English | American English |
| --- | --- |
| favour | |
| traveller | |
| cheque | |
| underground | |
| timetable | |

## b)  Discussion

Do you think that the differences between American and British English are
important? Do you think that the languages will get closer or grow further apart?

# 6  Writing

**Write about one of these:**
a)  English should be adopted officially as a world language.
b)  You have had a car accident. Describe it first in British English then rewrite
    it in American English.

# MODULE 1
## LANGUAGE C

## 1 Setting the scene

## 2 Vocabulary

| | |
|---|---|
| as a whole /ˈæz ə ˈhəul/ | all together |
| conform to /kənˈfɔːm tə/ | be the same as |
| variations /ˌveərɪˈeɪʃənz/ | differences |
| bred /bred/ | educated |
| tempo /ˈtempəu/ | speed |
| stretch /stretʃ/ | go a long way |
| remote /rɪˈməut/ | distant |
| diminutive /dɪˈmɪnjutɪv/ | word with a suffix indicating smallness |
| lane /leɪn/ | small street |
| wipe out /waɪp aut/ | destroy completely |

## 3 Tape

The speaker on the tape is talking about his native dialect. While you are listening to him the first time, pick out the answers to the following questions:
a)  Where in Britain does the speaker come from?
b)  What is the most striking feature of his native accent?
c)  Which language was the original basis of his dialect?

# 4 Language study

### a) Vocabulary and pronunciation: place names

The text mentioned many British place names. As is often the case, it is difficult to guess the pronunciation from the spelling. Here is a list of the major ones. Underline the stressed syllable in each one:

| | |
|---|---|
| Birmingham | Liverpool |
| Sheffield | Newcastle |
| the Pennine Hills | the Tyne |
| Mount Cheviot | Northumberland |
| Alnwick | Durham |
| Edinburgh | Ayrshire |
| Aberdeen | |

### b) Useful words and phrases

Note that in the above list, there are eight towns, two counties, one mountain, one river and one mountain range. Which of them use the definite article? The use of 'the' with place names in English has regular rules and few exceptions. Put the following names into the correct category, using the definite article where appropriate:

*Thames / Everest / USA / Andes / Middle East / Tate Gallery / Rockies / Hilton / Smithsonian / Rhine / Kilimanjaro / Lebanon / Ganges / Louvre / Senegal / USSR / Pyrenees / Ben Nevis / K2 / Zambezi*

| Buildings | Countries | Rivers |
|---|---|---|
| | | |
| | | |

| Mountains | Mountain Ranges |
|---|---|
| | |
| | |

### c) Language focus: intensifying adverbs

The speaker says that some people in Wales speak 'a *completely different* language'. We use an adverb as an 'intensifier' to modify an adjective. Look at the following list, ranked roughly by degree (there are many more):

absolutely
completely
extremely
terribly
dead (informal)
unusually
surprisingly
very
pretty (informal)
rather (often used with a negative sense)
fairly
quite (with an 'absolute" adjective such as 'perfect' or 'wrong', it means
   'absolutely')

**d) Activity**

For each sentence below, give an opposite opinion, using one of the intensifiers given above, and one of the adjectives from the following list. The first one has been done for you.

*lucky / interesting / repulsive / refreshing / tasteless / chilly / brilliant / tedious / exciting / difficult*

1 'That was boring!' — 'Really? I found it <u>extremely interesting</u>'
2 'It's quite warm today.' — 'I'm afraid I disagree. I think it's _____ _____ for the time of year.'
3 'What a dull party!' — 'Never! I thought it was _____ _____.'
4 'What a charming man!' — 'Do you think so? I find him _____ _____.'
5 'This is fun!' — 'Get away! It's _____ _____!'
6 'This exercise is easy!' — 'You must be joking! It's _____ _____.
7 'He deserved to win'. — 'No he didn't; he was just _____ _____.'
8 'This cake is quite nice.' — 'Nice! it's _____ _____!'
9 'Picasso was a rotten painter'. — 'What? He was _____ _____!'
10 'Camping is a silly way to spend a holiday'. — 'Rubbish! I think it's _____ _____.'

# 5 Transfer

**a) Tape**

Listen to the tape again and find the answers to the following:

1 Which area does the dialect used in books and on the BBC come from?
2 What are the big city dialects based on?
3 How old is the speaker?
4 What does the dialect word 'laddie' mean?
5 Is the word 'neddy' a dialect word?
6 How do Northumbrians say 'cry'?
7 Where did the Saxons settle?
8 How many copies of the Lallans Bible have been sold?

**b) Discussion**

The economic and political history of Britain has had a major influence on the dialect which is now considered standard. How has the course of history affected your native language? Are some dialects regarded as better than others?

# 6 Writing

**Write about one of these:**
a) Describe the main variations in the way your language is spoken in different parts of the country.
b) Do you think that local dialects or languages should be preserved or allowed to disappear?

## 1 Setting the scene

PITY YOU WERE OUT FOR A DUCK, OLD FRUIT!

## 2 Vocabulary

| | |
|---|---|
| snob /snob/ | class-conscious person |
| posh /poʃ/ | upper-class |
| public school /ˈpʌblɪk ˈskul/ | expensive private school |
| mess up /ˈmes ʌp/ | put into confusion |
| thread /θred/ | connecting line of a story |
| deflated /dɪˈfleɪtɪd/ | made to feel smaller |
| squirm /skwɜːm/ | move about with embarrassment |
| lilt /lɪlt/ | rhythm |
| gift /gɪft/ | special ability |
| facet /ˈfæset/ | aspect, area |

## 3 Tape

On the tape you will hear an Englishman talking about the way foreigners speak English. While you are listening to him, find the answers to the following questions:

a) Why does the speaker want foreigners to speak with their own accent?
b) How can a foreigner speaking with a 'genuine' British accent be amusing?
c) Why was Petula Clark popular in France?

12

# 4  Language study

### a)  Vocabulary and pronunciation: negative prefixes

Underline the stressed syllables in the following words, and give their opposites (underlining the stressed syllable again). The first one has been done for you.

| <u>com</u>fortable | un<u>com</u>fortable |
| recognisable | |
| perfect | |
| attractive | |
| interesting | |
| ordinary | |
| intelligibility | |
| understand | |
| meaningful | |
| reasonable | |

### b)  Useful words and phrases: colour idioms

The speaker says he was 'tickled pink' (very pleased) to be taken for a Frenchman. Many colours are associated with feelings or moods in English. Fill in the gaps in the following sentences with the appropriate colour from the list given:

*red / purple / blue / black / yellow / green / white*

1  When she saw my fur coat she was _____ with envy.
2  Since losing his job he has been in a mood of _____ despair.
3  When he realised the danger he went _____ with fear.
4  The boss gets furious with latecomers: he really sees _____.
5  When he saw the mess he went _____ with rage.
6  I knew he hadn't got the guts to tell her: he's really _____.
7  It's freezing. I'm _____ with cold.

### c)  Language focus: modals + perfect infinitive

'The Frenchman *could have spent* more time on broadening his vocabulary.' Modals (must, may, might, should, ought to, need (to), can, could, would) have no perfect form, but take 'have' + past participle to refer to past events. Some of them, out of context, may be ambiguous. For example, the speaker clearly means that the Frenchman did not spend more time on broadening his vocabulary, but that it was possible. On its own, the sentence could mean that it is possible that he did, but not at all sure. Likewise, 'he should have' and 'he ought to have' can mean either that it is likely that he did, or that he was morally obliged to, but didn't.

### d)  Activity

Rewrite the following sentences to refer to the past, using the adverbial where given:

1  It must be freezing. (last night)

_____

2  He should be there by now. (an hour ago)

_____

3  I think you ought to tell your mother before you go.

_____

4  It can't be Fred: he isn't at home.

_____

5  You could give us a hand with the clearing up. (after the party)

_____

6  You needn't bother; it isn't difficult. (There are two possibilities here — what is the difference in meaning?)

_____

7  I'd like to leave before the end but it's embarrassing. (!)

_____

8  You might enjoy the party if you came.

_____

9  Researchers may find a cure for AIDS. (already)

_____

10  He's setting off at midday, so he ought to arrive by five.

_____

# Transfer

### a)  Tape
Listen again to the tape and for the first section, find the best answer to the following:

1  The speaker only feels comfortable with
a)  posh people.
b)  people with good accents.
c)  people whose accents he recognises.
d)  people from Liverpool.

2  He prefers
a)  French people.
b)  foreigners with accents.
c)  foreigners who understand cricket.
d)  foreigners who understand jokes.

3  He finds foreign accents
a)  interesting.
b)  ordinary.
c)  difficult to explain.
d)  amusing.

In the second section, say whether the following statements are true or false:

| | |
|---|---|
| 1  The speaker doesn't mind how strong an accent is. | T/F |
| 2  He thinks most foreigners have quite a strong accent. | T/F |
| 3  He feels that most foreigners are quite happy to speak with an accent. | T/F |

In the third section, fill in the gaps in the following sentences from what the speaker says:
1  He feels deflated when someone _____ that he's English.
2  Maurice Chevalier was a _____ French speaker of English.
3  We should accept a wider _____ of accents.

### b)  Discussion
Is there a 'correct' way of speaking English? Is there a 'correct' way of speaking your language? Should people be encouraged to speak a language in one way?

# 6  Writing

**Write about one of these:**
a)  A person's language reflects his or her personality.
b)  Write a short thank-you letter to
    i)  a close friend.
    ii)  an important person you do not know well.

# MODULE 2
## LAW AND ORDER A

## 1   Setting the scene

## 2   Vocabulary

| | | |
|---|---|---|
| entrepreneur *n* | (1.8) | a man who sets up and organises a business |
| target *n* | (1.20) | place selected for burglary |
| antiques *n pl* | (1.23) | old and valuable goods e.g. furniture, jewellery, etc |
| dispose of *v phr* | (1.28) | get rid of, sell |
| loot *n* | (1.28) | valuable stolen objects |
| legitimate *adj* | (1.30) | legal |
| tip-off *n* | (1.34) | piece of helpful information |
| meticulous *adj* | (1.68) | very careful |
| haul *n* | (1.76) | stolen goods |
| Crown Court *n phr* | (1.102) | British law court for more serious criminal cases |
| occupational hazard *n phr* | (1.105) | risk connected with a particular type of work |

## 3   Text

While reading the text, find the answers to the following questions:
a)   What type of target premises does Martin Hutton specialise in?
b)   What type of target premises does Dennis Richards specialise in?
c)   What plans does Harry Bryant make before a burglary?

# ■ ANATOMY OF BURGLARY

Martin Hutton, 32, has an average annual income of £75,000. He lives with his wife in a £250-a-week flat in London's West End, drives a new Mercedes and takes holidays in The Bahamas. His neighbours believe he is a successful entrepreneur in a growth industry — electronics, perhaps. Certainly he is successful and in a growth industry — but not electronics. Martin Hutton is a burglar. He belongs to an elite minority — perhaps 3% of all burglars — who plan crimes in every detail and take pride in their skills. As he puts it: 'There's a world of difference between me and your average half-brick and screwdriver man.'

Martin Hutton specialises in country houses. Before approaching his targets, he reads about them in libraries and studies pictures in county magazines to find out what antiques they contain. 'I might spend up to a week researching a property,' he says. 'Before I arrive at the target I generally know exactly what I'll be taking.' He disposes of his loot through a professional receiver — a fence — who runs a legitimate business as a front. Hutton receives only about one-third of the true market value of the goods, but the fence, with his network of contacts, offers him a bonus tip-off about suitable targets.

Hutton is just one of thousands of men — there are very few women burglars — who steal more than £200-million-worth from private homes each year. Burglary has been one of Britain's fastest-growing crimes, and has now reached the level where one home in England and Wales is hit every 35 seconds. Many go unreported. A recent report puts the chance of your home being burgled this year at one in 25. While cash remains the burglar's prime target, electronic equipment is highly prized. 'There is far more temptation for burglars than ten years ago,' explains Surrey's CID chief Vincent McFadden. 'Nearly every home contains goods worth stealing — televisions, video recorders, hi-fi systems, computers.'

Two researchers from the University of Cambridge Institute of Criminology recently interviewed more than 300 convicted burglars around southern England. From their research three main types of burglar were identified, with men like Martin Hutton at the top of the tree. The burglar who breaks into your home is more likely to resemble Dennis Richards, 24, who makes an average £20,000 a year and lives with a girlfriend in a rented house in Bristol. His planning is less meticulous than Hutton's. 'I usually keep places under surveillance for a day or so, noting what times people enter and leave, and familiarising myself with routes for a quick escape.' His burglaries, like some 80% of the total, are always from unoccupied premises. He sells his hauls through a middleman, a retired burglar, who takes 15% as 'commission'.

Two-thirds of all burglars in Britain are under 21 — like Harry Bryant, the third type identified by the research team. Aged 18, Harry lives with his parents in a Manchester council house and commits most of his crimes when he is drunk. His hauls, like those in nine out of ten burglaries, are usually worth less than £500, and he 'earns' between £5000 and £10,000 a year. 'I don't bother with planning,' he confesses. 'If I see a promising place — no sign of life, no peeping neighbours — I just smash a window.' Pubs are his best market for stolen goods. 'Spread the word around a pub, and you'll soon unload the lot,' he says. But such deals with strangers expose him to the risk of betrayal; he blames potential customers for his six arrests. For the 25,000 or so burglars who are convicted each year, the maximum sentence is 14 years, but even for cases serious enough to go before a Crown Court the average is only 15½ months — a punishment regarded by many as merely an occupational hazard. Says Surrey CID chief Vincent McFadden: 'Light sentences have reduced fear of punishment and almost certainly contributed to the burglary boom.'

*(From Reader's Digest © 1985; article by Leslie Watkins and Lois Fletcher)*

16

# 4 Language study

## a) Vocabulary: criminal actions

The table below is divided into three parts:

actor — action — object/person

Complete the table using the words given. Use each word only once.

*court / disposes of / steals / burglar / fence / sentences / loot / arrest*

| Actor | Action | Object/Person |
|---|---|---|
| burglar | | antiques |
| | receives | |
| middleman | | haul |
| police | | |
| | | burglar |

## b) Useful words and phrases

The following phrases all deal with numerical expressions. Check that you know their meaning.

— a £250-a-week flat
— £2 million worth
— every 35 seconds
— one in 25
— an average £20,000 a year
— nine out of ten burglaries

Now rewrite the following sentences, adapting one of the phrases above. The first one has been done for you.

1  Mr X earns about £50,000 a year.
   Mr X earns an average £50,000 a year.

2  He lives in a London flat which costs £1200 a month.

3  10 per cent of his clients are rich and powerful.

4  Mr X is a busy and successful man. He can only accept one new job a month.
   Mr X earns an average £50,000 a year.

5  He invested £2 million from his personal savings in the enterprise.

## c) Language focus: prepositions after nouns and verbs

The text contains a number of:

• noun + preposition combinations
• verb + preposition combinations
• verbs without prepositions

Look at the list below.

| Noun + preposition | Verb + preposition | Verb without preposition |
|---|---|---|
| pride in | to specialise in | to approach |
| difference between | to dispose of | to resemble |
| ... and ... | to expose s.o. to | to research |
| chance of | to belong to | to enter |
| temptation for | to bother with | to leave |
| top of | to contribute to | to reach |
| no sign of | to arrive at/in | |
| market for | | |
| risk of | | |
| fear of | | |

**d) Activity**

Complete the following text by writing an appropriate preposition, where necessary.

The risk (1)_____ burglary to big-city homes is greater than to blocks of flats. Although it is easy to enter (2)_____ blocks of flats, burglars often dislike them because of the fear (3)_____ being caught without an escape route. 'You could be on the tenth floor. If someone comes in, it's not so easy to leave (4)_____ the flat by jumping out of the window!' Burglars looking for a target prefer houses which they can approach (5)_____ with little chance (6)_____ being seen by neighbours. There is a big difference (7)_____ the highly professional burglar who specialises (8)_____ jewellery and works of art and the casual burglar who doesn't bother (9)_____ any planning or research. Both types dispose (10)_____ their haul in different ways — the former through a fence; the latter through friends or strangers.

# 5  Transfer

**a)  Text**

Complete the table of information about the three types of burglars in the text.

|  | **Martin Hutton** | **Dennis Richards** | **Harry Bryant** |
|---|---|---|---|
| Average annual income |  |  |  |
| Accommodation |  |  |  |
| Approximate research time |  |  |  |
| Disposal channel |  |  |  |

**b)  Discussion**

To what extent is burglary from private homes a problem in your country/city? What precautions can people take to reduce the risk of burglary?

# 6  Writing

**Write about one of these:**

a)   Write a detailed report of a crime you have witnessed.

b)   The best place to develop one's skill as a criminal is in prison.

# MODULE 2
## LAW AND ORDER B

## 1   Setting the scene

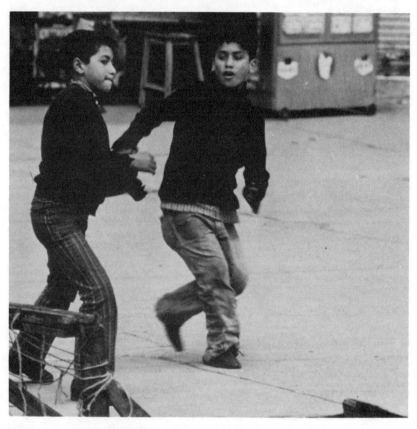

## 2   Vocabulary

| | | |
|---|---|---|
| marginal *n/adj* | | poor person existing on the edge of society |
| prostitute *n* | (l.1) | person who provides sex for money |
| solitary *adj* | (l.3) | alone |
| layabout *n* | (l.4) | lazy person who avoids working |
| petty thief *n phr* | (l.4) | thief who steals things of little value |
| Municipality *n* | (l.13) | city or the people who govern it |
| pocket money *n phr* | (l.15) | money given weekly to a child |
| pickpocket *vi/n* | (l.22) | steal things from people's pockets |
| cell *n* | (l.27) | small room in a prison |
| pardon *vt* | (l.33) | forgive |

## 3   Text

The following text is extracted from the autobiography of Miguel Duran, one of the urban poor living in Cali, the third largest city in Colombia with a population of over a million. While reading the text, find answers to the following questions:
a)   Was Miguel older or younger than the other thieves in the Central Market?
b)   Did Miguel accept his father's offer of work?
c)   When was the best time of day for pickpocketing?

# ■ AUTOBIOGRAPHY OF AN URBAN MARGINAL

So, by the time I was eight years old, I was going round with a prostitute. I was a gamin (the Colombian colloquialism for 'street urchin'), though I was more a solitary type than a member of any regular gang. I was just a layabout. I saw other petty thieves who were big — sixteen year olds and
5 twelve year olds — and of course I wanted to do the same as them. I wanted to get a room to live in; at that time rooms were cheap — six pesos for a night. Then Eneas (the prostitute) asked me if I would like to live with her and I said yes. So I went to my father and told him I wasn't coming back to the house again. My father asked me why I wasn't going to school and I told him that
10 I was drinking and smoking cigarettes. And my father said, 'All right, you go where you like and I'll close the house.' Then I told him that I had become a petty thief and had a woman, and he put his hand on his head. 'What I'm going to do with you is this; as I work for the Municipality, I'm going to give you to the Municipality so that you can sweep up and carry things in the workshop.
15 I'll buy you a pair of trousers and a shirt every week, and I'll give you pocket money to go to the cinema.' And I said 'Father, I don't need it, look,' and I took piles of money out of my pocket. I told him again that I wasn't coming back and I left.

Why were those people so dumb? It was easy to rob. Those people (rural
20 migrants to the city) came to open their eyes here in Cali. They were incredibly dumb and humble. At midday you could rob people like crazy around the Central Market. So I went to live with Eneas and I started pickpocketing. Eneas told me to go and work with a man called Madra, so we worked together. He would push and shove people in the street and I would stick my
25 hand into their pockets and steal things. Then the police hit me — pow — and they took me to the police station. They searched me and — pow — to the cells — the 'Pavilion of Minors'. I was about 10 years old then and as it was a first offence, they let me out after a few days. So I changed profession and I became a caimanero (someone who steals from ladies' handbags). You work
30 with a partner who gets ahead of the woman, then stops, and when she tries to get round him, you come up behind her and — pow — you hit her and grab her handbag. So I stole like crazy till they got me again. And they put me in that pigsty, the Pavilion of Minors, and then they wouldn't pardon me again, and they sent me to the Reformatory near Buga, about 75 kilometres north of
35 Cali. From then on I stopped using my proper name and started using a variety of false names. I escaped and eventually I got back to Eneas in Cali.

Eneas was about 19 and was a hell of a thief. We had great times with her. I went back to stealing, and the next day the police got me again, and — pow — into the Pavilion of Minors — and — pow — back to the Reformatory in
40 Buga. There they caned me and shaved my head and took my clothes. Eventually I escaped again, but in escaping I twisted my arm, and my elbow became swollen. I managed to get back to Cali and I went to Eneas and she bathed the arm in hot water. Then, after two days, they put her in jail for five to ten years for attacking and wounding someone. I sold all my things and hers
45 to pay the rent, and I went back to thieving. Eventually I moved to a different lodging. I must have been about 14 then. In the next room there was a black woman from Choco who had run away from her husband. She cured my arm, though it's left permanently bent. She was hard-working and sold in the Market; I would steal cases of tomatoes for her to sell. Then her husband
50 came and took her away, and I was left alone, living from theft. Soon I was caught and sent to the Reformatory again.

*(From Casual Work and Poverty in Third World Cities by Ray Bronley and Chris Gerry)*

# 4 Language study

## a) Vocabulary: verbs of force

The following verbs deal with different actions involving force, some of them criminal. Link the verb on the left with its definition on the right.

| | **Verb** | | **Definition** |
|---|---|---|---|
| 1 | rob | a) | take hold of (something) with a sudden violent movement |
| 2 | wound | b) | push violently |
| 3 | thieve | c) | take away (something) unlawfully |
| 4 | cane | d) | act as a thief |
| 5 | shove | e) | use violence against (someone) |
| 6 | twist | f) | hit with a piece of wood |
| 7 | grab | g) | injure |
| 8 | steal | h) | take away from someone property unlawfully |
| 9 | attack | i) | injure (a limb) by turning (it) violently |

## b) Useful words and phrases: American v. British English

The text includes a number of words/expressions more commonly associated with American English:

| American English | British English |
|---|---|
| regular | normal, ordinary |
| dumb | stupid |
| like crazy | very much |
| a hell of a . . . | a very good . . . |

## c) Language focus: verb + '–ing' v. infinitive with 'to'

The text contains a number of verbs which may be followed by either of the above forms.
In **type 1** below the meaning is totally changed by the choice of form;
in **type 2** there is only a slight change of meaning;
in **type 3** there is no systematic difference.

Look at the following pairs of sentences:

**Type 1**
— She asked me if I would like to live with her. (offer)
— She asked me if I liked living with her. (if I enjoyed . . .)
— I stopped using my proper name. (I used another name)
— I stopped to rest my elbow. (in order to)
**Type 2**
— She tries to get round him. (attempts)
— She tries getting round him. (experiments)
**Type 3**
— I started using a variety of false names.
— I started to use a variety of false names.

## d) Activity

Complete the following sentences using the verb in brackets either in the 'ing' form or as an infinitive with 'to'.

I remember (see) (1)_____ a TV programme recently about a criminal who talked about trying (renounce) (2)_____ his life of crime. He admitted that he hated (be stuck) (3)_____ in the vicious circle of crime and jail, and really regretted (spend) (4)_____ so much of his life behind bars. But he said that he'd always enjoyed (fraternise) (5)_____ with other petty thieves — and in fact didn't know anyone outside the criminal world. One day, while spending a short spell in jail, he decided that he would prefer (give up) (6)_____ the easy money of petty crime. The problem was how to do it. When he was released he purposely forgot (visit) (7)_____ his normal pubs, although he would have loved (meet) (8)_____ his old pals. Then he tried (move) (9)_____ to another neighbourhood to escape temptation altogether, and finally got himself a menial job. He said that for all the tedium of a 9 to 5 existence he enjoyed (live) <u>(10)</u>_____ in society rather than outside it.

# 5  Transfer

**a)  Text**

The table below shows Miguel's progress in the criminal world. From the details in the text fill in the missing information.

| Age | Criminal activity | Partner Yes/No | Caught Yes/No | Released/escaped |
|-----|-------------------|----------------|---------------|------------------|
| 8 | | No | | — |
| | Pickpocket | | | |
| | Handbag thief | | | Escaped |
| 14 | | No | | ? |

**b)  Discussion**

Petty theft is as much a problem in rich countries as in poor countries, but are the motives different? What types of petty theft are common in your country?

# 6  Writing

**Write about one of these:**

a)  You have been caught by the police for speeding. Write a letter to the police explaining why you were driving over the speed limit.

b)  Poverty leads to crime.

# MODULE 2
## LAW AND ORDER C

## 1  Setting the scene

## 2  Vocabulary

| | |
|---|---|
| tights /taɪts/ | women's and girls' close fitting garment covering the legs and lower part of the body |
| charge /tʃɑːdʒ/ | accusation |
| summary trial /ˈsʌmərɪ traɪəl/ | a trial in a magistrates' court |
| submission /sʌbˈmɪʃən/ | other points of view to be considered |
| try /traɪ/ | examine in a law court |
| plead /pliːd/ | answer a charge in court |
| conviction /kənˈvɪkʃən/ | occasions when found guilty |
| bail /beɪl/ | release from custody on an instruction to return to court on a given date at a set time |
| impulse /ˈɪmpʌls/ | sudden wish |
| mar /mɑː/ | spoil |

## 3  Tape

The listening passage you are going to hear is a court case in a magistrates' court — the court which deals with minor criminal offences in the UK. This court is a people's court in the sense that magistrates are members of the community, normally without any legal training, but advised on points of law by a court clerk.

While you are listening to the tape, find the answers to the following questions:

a)   What offence is the defendant charged with?

b)   What is the name of the higher court by whom the defendant may choose to be tried?

c)   Does the court accept the defendant's offer to pay the fine off at £5 per week?

# 4 Language study

## a) Vocabulary and pronunciation: the legal process

The table below deals with key figures and actions in the legal process.
First underline the syllable which carries the word stress in the nouns and verbs.
Then match the person on the left with the most appropriate action or role in the other columns.
The first one is 1 c) v).

| | | | | | | |
|---|---|---|---|---|---|---|
| 1 | the defendant | a) | decide | i) | the details of the offence |
| 2 | the prosecutor | b) | advises | ii) | the defendant |
| 3 | the solicitor | c) | pleads | iii) | the justices |
| 4 | the justices | d) | defends | iv) | the penalty |
| 5 | the court clerk | e) | presents | v) | guilty |

## b) Language focus: passive reported statements with introductory 'it' and subject raising

1  The normal statement word order is subject + verb,
eg  You stole a pair of tights.
However, when the subject is a clause, the position of the subject clause is usually changed,
eg  It is said that you stole a pair of tights.
The subject clause is moved to the end of the sentence, and the subject position is filled by the introductory 'it'.
The new sentence contains two subjects:
  i)  'it' — the introductory subject with no meaning.
  ii)  'that you stole a pair of tights' — the postponed subject.

Here are some more examples from the tape:
— It is decided that their powers of punishment are insufficient.
— It is alleged that she saw the defendant pick up a pair of tights.
— It is stressed that they have agreed to keep her on.
— It is suggested that she is dealt with by way of financial penalty.
— It is agreed that she would pay any fine that you may impose.

2  An extension to the above rule is called 'subject raising',
eg  You are said to have stolen a pair of tights.
Here the subject of the subject clause is raised to the subject position of the main verb. The subject clause, left without a subject, must have its verb turned into an infinitive.
  i)  'you' — subject raised from subject clause to subject of main verb
  ii)  'are said' — main verb
  iii)  'to have stolen' — perfect infinitive form since the verb has lost its subject

Here are some examples from the tape:
— She is then claimed to have walked out of the shop.
— The tights are understood to have been recovered.
— A higher sum is felt to be reasonable.

The tense of the infinitive depends on the relationship between the tense of the main verb and the tense of the subject clause verb.
Where the tense of the subject clause verb = tense of the main verb, use the present infinitive.
Where the tense of the subject clause verb is past in relation to tense of the main verb, use the present perfect infinitive.

It is felt that a higher sum is reasonable.
A higher sum is felt to be reasonable.

It was felt that a higher sum was reasonable.
A higher sum was felt to be reasonable.

It is felt that a higher sum was reasonable.
A higher sum is felt to have been reasonable.

It was felt that a higher sum had been reasonable.
A higher sum was felt to have been reasonable.

### c) Activity

Rewrite the following sentences in the passive, beginning your sentences with the word(s) given. The first one has been done for you.

1　We believe the defendant entered the house by climbing in through a bedroom window.
　It is believed that the defendant entered the house by climbing in through a bedroom window.

2　It is thought that he brought a ladder with him.
　He _____.

3　We suggest that the defendant had an accomplice with him.
　It _____.

4　We don't believe the accomplice entered the house.
　The accomplice _____.

5　The owners reported to the police that many valuable items of jewellery had been stolen.
　Many valuable items of jewellery _____.

6　However, we feel that the owners helped the burglar.
　However, it _____.

7　It is believed that the whole burglary was organised by the owners.
　The whole burglary _____.

8　Our reason for thinking this is that we understand the owners made an exaggerated insurance claim.
　Our reason for thinking this is that the owners _____.

9　We consider that this insurance claim is fraudulent.
　This insurance claim _____.

10　We think the owners left the country when they heard about our investigations.
　The owners _____.

# 5　Transfer

### a) Tape

Complete the following form which the court clerk wrote during the trial:

Case Number: _____

Defendant's name: Michelle Young _____

Defendant's address: 30 Highfields Close, Cambridge _____

Date of birth: _____

Charge: _____

Date of alleged theft: _____

Value of goods stolen: _____

Mode of trial: _____

Defendant's plea: _____

Earnings after tax: _____

Fine imposed: _____

Payment per week: _____

**b) Discussion**

The justices (judges) who sit in the magistrates' courts are not legally trained, although they are advised by a legally trained court clerk. They are members of the community who are felt to be in a better position to judge the minor crimes which come before them. Do you have a similar system in your country? What do you consider to be the advantages or disadvantages of such a system?

# 6 Writing

**Write about one of these:**

a) Describe a criminal trial in your country.
b) Only harsher penalties will reduce the crime rate.

# MODULE 2
## LAW AND ORDER D

## 1   Setting the scene

PARAMOUNT PICTURES PRESENTS

**The Godfather**

## 2   Vocabulary

| | |
|---|---|
| emergence /ɪˈmɜːdʒəns/ | appearance |
| despotic /desˈpotɪk/ | unjust or cruel use of power |
| alienate /ˈeɪlɪəneɪt/ | make an enemy of someone |
| reprisal /rɪˈpraɪzəl/ | punishment |
| syndicated /ˈsɪndɪkeɪtɪd/ | combined together for a particular purpose, especially making money |
| thrive /θraɪv/ | be successful |
| commission /kəˈmɪʃən/ | group of people appointed to perform certain duties |
| illicit /ɪˈlɪsət/ | illegal |
| assimilate /əˈsɪmɪleɪt/ | become part of a group, race, country, etc |

## 3   Tape

The taped passage you are going to hear deals with the Mafia. The speaker describes the origins, development and organisation of this group. While you are listening, answer the following questions:

a)   What was the basis of the Mafia's code of justice?
b)   What name did the American branch of the Mafia adopt?
c)   What is the function of the lieutenants?

# 4 Language study

## a) Vocabulary and pronunciation: power and authority

The following words, taken from the tape, deal with the area of power and authority. First complete the word table. Then underline the syllable which carries the word stress.

| Action | System | Person |
|---|---|---|
| manage | | |
| administer | | |
| | government | |
| | oppression | |
| | | leader |
| | | dictator |

## b) Useful words and phrases: adverbs of degree

Adverbs of degree can be divided into those whose meaning can be thought of in terms of a *scale* eg very, fairly, and those whose meaning can be thought of in terms of a *limit* (or end-point of a scale) eg completely.

Indicate in the table below whether the adverbs are scale or limit. The first one has been done for you.

| Adverb | Scale | Limit |
|---|---|---|
| gradually | √ | |
| totally | | |
| partly | | |
| absolutely | | |
| largely | | |
| mainly | | |
| altogether | | |
| steadily | | |
| only | | |

## c) Language focus: increase and decrease

The speaker uses a number of verbs to indicate the ideas of increase and decrease. These verbs can be divided into transitive and intransitive. Some can be used in both cases.

| Transitive | Intransitive |
|---|---|
| to increase (with countable ideas) | to increase |
| to raise<br>to extend<br>to grow* | to rise<br>to extend<br>to grow |
| to diminish<br>to decrease (with countable ideas)<br>to reduce | to diminish<br>to decrease<br>to fall<br>to reduce |

*transitive use with another meaning, eg to grow flowers

**d) Activity**

Indicate the line on the graph which refers to each of the sentences below by writing the number of the sentence in the box beside the line on the graph.

*Number of Prisoners*

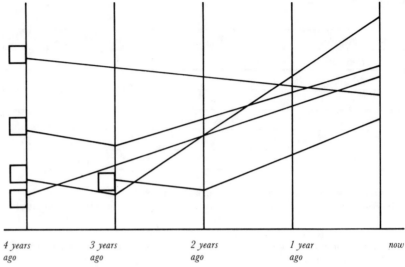

| 4 years ago | 3 years ago | 2 years ago | 1 year ago | now |

1  Four years ago the number of prisoners fell slightly, but since then it has increased steadily.

2  Four years ago the number of prisoners decreased slightly, but since then it has risen dramatically.

3  Since the government raised the minimum penalty for theft four years ago, the number of prisoners has fallen slightly.

4  Four years ago the prison population started to grow steadily, and it has continued to grow at the same rate since then.

5  Although we managed to reduce the prison population three years ago, our attempts to decrease it further have been unsuccessful since then.

Now complete the following sentences by using an appropriate word derived from the word given in brackets.

We have become (increase) (1)_____ concerned about the rapid (grow) (2)_____ of crime over the last few years. Despite (extend) (3)_____ efforts we have been unable to prevent a (rise) (4)_____ trend in most areas of the country, and with the (reduce) (5)_____ in police I expect this trend to continue.

# Transfer

**a)  Tape**

Complete the following profile of the Mafia. Fill in the table:

| The Mafia |
|---|
| Origins — when: _____ |
| — where: _____ |
| Attempt to reduce Mafia power — when: _____ |
| Was the attempt successful?  YES/PARTLY/NO |
| Era of migration to the US: _____ |
| Period of greatest power |
| in organised crime in the US: _____ |
| Major illegal operations: _____ |

Complete the organisation tree:

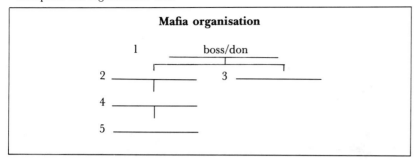

**Mafia organisation**

1 _____ boss/don

2 _____   3 _____

4 _____

5 _____

### b)  Discussion

Do you think criminal activity is normal in an unjust society? Is there likely to be less crime if everyone is equal? Was Robin Hood justified in robbing the rich to give to the poor? Can crime ever be justified?

# 6  Writing

**Write about one of these:**

a)  Write a letter to a newspaper explaining why you think the police should receive higher pay.

b)  We are all born criminals, but most of us learn to control our behaviour.

# MODULE 3
## EDUCATION A

## 1 Setting the scene

## 2 Vocabulary

| | |
|---|---|
| comprehensive school *n* (l.7) *phr* | school for all children from the age of 11 to 16 or 18 |
| short of *prep phr* (l.11) | not having enough of |
| PTA *abbrev* (l.15) | Parents and Teachers Association — a group of interested parents and teachers who help the school |
| high school *n* (l.18) | may now be a comprehensive school, but originally like a grammar school |
| funds *n* (l.20) | money for a special purpose |
| lack *vt* (l.25) | not have |
| grammar school *n* (l.38) | school for academic children, with an entrance exam |
| maintained school *n* (l.41) | school supported by state money |
| fees *n* (l.42) | money paid for going to the school |
| public school *n* (l.44) | private school |

## 3 Text

While you are reading the passage, find the answers to the following questions as briefly as possible:

a) How many different types of secondary school are there in England?

b) What is the biggest problem for the schools today?

c) What are the different ways that people are trying to solve this problem?

# ■ A CRISIS IN EDUCATION

Bankfield County High School in Cheshire was built in the early sixties, and the buildings have that peculiarly depressed appearance of uncared-for modern architecture that has been allowed to rot and decay. Cheshire has allotted no money for decoration since 1979, so, in the summer of 1985, the new headmaster of Bankfield bought his own paint and paintbrush and tackled his dingy study himself. But even an energetic head cannot maintain an entire comprehensive school. Morale in the school is remarkably high, but Bankfield is being run on the principles of 'muddling through', 'making do': admirable British virtues, but unlikely to prepare future citizens for a high-technology society where only the most skilled will survive.

Bankfield is short of computers, it's short of equipment for physics and electronics (although dedicated teachers, contrary to popular image, have spent many voluntary hours constructing home-made kits for practical science work), and, at a basic level, the school is very short of books. Recently the head asked the PTA to buy one set of crucial textbooks needed for a public exam, but the chairman of the PTA explained that it was difficult to ask unemployed and hard-pressed parents to contribute.

At Weaversham County High School, in prosperous mid-Cheshire, parents have confronted the crisis in an uncompromising, vigorous way, and they now contribute about £10,000 to £12,000 a year directly to school funds. The money is collected through a sophisticated covenant system under a school trust which has a charitable status and gets tax relief on income. The days of the jumble sale and the PTA dance are far behind — this is major-league fund-raising, and the headmaster has reluctantly accepted it as part of his job.

The 'unofficial' money pays for many of the things that Bankfield lacks; £3000 has just been spent equipping a microtech lab, there are numerous computers, and most of the corridors gleam with new paint.

The headmaster says that some of the parents are unable to contribute and that others refuse on moral grounds, but the majority are able and willing to pay for some of their children's state education. However, it is recognised in some quarters that massive parental contributions at some schools are creating inequalities between the different comprehensives.

Nationally, parents' contributions to secondary schools rose by 170% between 1981 and 1986, and one wonders how long it will be before one energetic group bids to take over a comprehensive school completely, or 'privatise' it and run it independently.

It was parental initiative that brought about the creation of the independent Grange Grammar School at Hartford in Cheshire in 1978. Then the school had 27 pupils. By 1986, it had 380, with an ever-increasing number of candidates for the entrance exam. The school developed over precisely the same period when the maintained schools were finding themselves coping with dwindling resources. Fees at the Grange for 1986 were nearly £500 a term, and the school had a £1 million turnover. The atmosphere is workmanlike, not luxurious; the Grange doesn't pretend to enjoy the traditions or facilities of an ancient public school, but the staff wear gowns and the children learn Latin.

The headmaster denies that the school is socially elitist, and points to the sacrifices made by the parents to pay the fees: 'The holiday on the Costa del Sol isn't going to take place this year and the Volvo is going to run into its seventh year.' The headmaster and the parents seem to agree that the main attraction is that the Grange recreates the system of the old-fashioned grammar school: structured teaching, discipline, hard work, good manners are features which are reassuringly familiar.

Educationists may argue about how relevant all this is to today's society, but there seems to be more and more consumer demand for private secondary schools. A London agency reported recently that inquiries about places had risen by 13% in the last year.

Still, in spite of the apparent boom in independent education, only six per cent of our children go to private schools. And most of the other 94% don't go to privately subsidised, maintained schools but rely on public funds to provide their education — funds which today often seem woefully inadequate. The headmaster of Bankfield High School speaks for those struggling against the odds. 'We have to believe it will get better, that people will realise that education is severely underfunded, and that the education of our children is the future of our nation.'

*(From The Listener, 20 April 1986;*
*article By Margaret Jay)*

# 4 Language study

### a) Vocabulary

The writer draws attention to the differences between the schools by his choice of words. Some of these words are given below. Sort them into two boxes, one for positive (+) and one for negative (−):

*depressed / prosperous / uncared-for / uncompromising / rot / vigorous / gleam / decay / sophisticated / dingy*

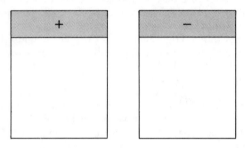

### b) Useful words and phrases

The following phrases occurred in the text. Use them again in a new context to complete the sentences below:

*being run / unlikely to / to take over / brought about / coping with / against the odds*

1  The directors are planning _____ two smaller rival firms.
2  Unless he improves his performance, he is _____ be promoted in the near future.
3  The teachers are having difficulty _____ the large increase in students.
4  The school shop is not _____ on a profit-making basis.
5  Although his chances of success are slight, he continues to fight _____.
6  The improvements were _____ by changes in school policy.

### c) Language focus: reported speech

This text uses a number of examples of reported speech. They fall into two categories. The first is a report of one statement made by a person:

The headmaster asked . . ./The chairman said . . .

The other is a more general statement which is still valid:

The head says that . . ./The parents deny that . . .

In the first category, the verb is in the past tense, with the following reported verb in the past, while in the second it is in the present.

### d) Activity

Change the following statement into reported speech, starting:

In his reply, the Minister stated that the government . . .

Minister: 'We hope that the new policy can be implemented as soon as possible. There are a number of changes to be made in the way in which schools are financed. Some schools have already piloted the scheme and it has been found to be much better than the old method. It has therefore been decided that all secondary schools will adopt the new methods as rapidly as possible, and by the end of the academic year all state schools will have made plans for adoption. We feel that the resultant changes will be of great benefit to schools and lead to substantial improvements in the system.'

## 5  Transfer

**a)  Text**

Read the passage and say whether the following statements are true or false:
1   Bankfield gets most of its money from parents.
2   The teachers at Bankfield work hard.
3   The children at Bankfield can learn a lot about modern technology.
4   Children at Weaversham have to pay a lot of money.
5   Most of the money is collected by jumble sales.
6   Few of the parents of Weaversham children are poor.
7   Grange school was started by parents.
8   Any child with enough money can go to Grange school.
9   All the parents at Grange school have Volvo cars.
10   The writer thinks that government does not spend enough money on schools.

**b)  Discussion**

How much do you have to pay to go to school in your country?
Are the schools run by the government?
If there are independent schools, are they better than the government schools?
Do you find it acceptable for wealthy parents to buy a superior education for their children?

## 6  Writing

**Write about one of these:**
a)   Education should be freely available to all.
b)   Describe the secondary education system in your country.

# MODULE 3
## EDUCATION B

## 1 Setting the scene

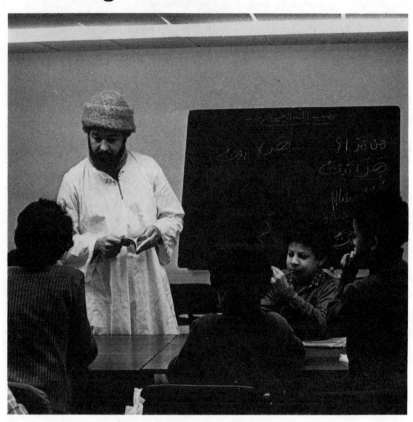

## 2 Key words and phrases

| | | |
|---|---|---|
| revelation *n* | (1.4) | something which shows the truth |
| guide *vt* | (1.6) | show the way |
| learn by heart *v phr* | (1.8) | learn completely so that you can repeat from memory |
| believer *n* | (1.8) | a person who believes in a religion (eg Buddhist, Christian) |
| faith *n* | (1.14) | strong belief |
| slate *n* | (1.23) | a flat piece of stone used to write on |
| revise *vt* | (1.23) | study again to prepare for a test |
| prompt *vt* | (1.24) | help someone to remember by repeating a word or phrase |
| recite *vt* | (1.30) | repeat a text without reading it |
| creed *n* | (1.63) | system of belief |

## 3 Text

As you are reading the text, find the answers to the following questions as briefly as possible:

a) What is the main purpose of a Qur'anic school?
b) How are Qur'anic schools supported?
c) What are the three main problems facing Qur'anic schools today?

# ■ QUR'ANIC SCHOOLS

The population of the Muslim world is currently estimated to be over 600 million, distributed largely in Africa and Asia and also in smaller groups in other parts of the world. For Muslims, the Qur'an is the divine revelation which the Prophet Mohammed was bidden to declare and to teach to all human beings all over the world at all times, in order that they should be guided in the right path in this and the other world.

The message had to be accurate to the letter, and in order to be transmitted to others it had to be learned by heart. The believers sat in a circle around the teacher and learned by listening, by repeating and by trying to understand. For women believers, the wives of the Prophet and their companions played an important role.

As time passed and the number of believers in Africa, Asia and other parts of the world increased, Islamic schools of various types were created. Backed by faith, these schools multiplied, flourished, developed and received financial and moral support from the people. To give a donation or help build a school was considered an act of piety. The fact that people have supported the Qur'anic educational movement spontaneously and uninterruptedly for almost fourteen centuries all over the vast Muslim world is a firm indication of the deeprooted-ness of the faith behind it.

The typical Qur'anic school usually has a single room; the number of students varies from ten or twenty to some hundreds. The teacher squats on a high platform orchestrating and watching the whole scene. Some students copy verses from the Holy Book onto a slate while others revise their assignments before being tested by the teacher or 'Sheikh'. Some are tested and prompted by monitors, boys older than themselves, before taking the final test. A small group in a corner read chapters in chorus with a leading boy. They correct themselves as they go along and the chorus continues until they have learned the passage. This method is very effective since every child is keen not to be out of tune and hence the concentration of attention, self-evaluation and self-correction. When a student can recite any part of the Qur'an from memory, he is given the title of 'Sheikh', a big celebration is held by the family and the teacher is given a valuable present.

Pedagogically, a number of practices are questionable, but some others are sound. It is worth noting that in the eighteenth century, two British educators, Andrew Bell and Joseph Lancaster, each independently adopted the monitor method from the Qur'anic schools of India. During the expansion of schools in England at that time, a very large number of students were taught using this method by a very small number of teachers. The monitor system is also known in France, probably as a result of long contact with North Africa. The practice of encouraging younger students to learn from older and more mature ones has much to recommend it.

In Qur'anic schools each student can proceed at his own pace. Some learn the Qur'an in two or three years, others need six or seven, while it is understood that some need not learn the whole text.

However, difficult problems have arisen, particularly in Africa and Asia. The Muslim world has been inundated by modern education on a European pattern and this has had a strong polarising effect on resources. Modern formal educa-tion is backed by practically the whole of the state educational budget while the Qur'anic schools are still maintained by private donations and impoverished trusts. Qur'anic schools in some countries occupy small overcrowded rooms with primitive equipment. The people sponsor the Qur'anic, the government promotes the formal schools.

In some countries, two or more streams of education exist, separated by an unbridgeable gap. This creates inequality of opportunity and influences currents of thought and prospects.

Difficulties also arise concerning the meaning and understanding of the texts, because of the difference between modern Arabic and the seventh century Arabic of the Qur'an.

But the most important problem today is the tension in some Muslim coun-tries between three types of language: the official language, which is either French or English, the vernacular, which is the mother tongue of everyday living, and the Arabic of Islam and the Qur'an. To be torn between three very important options, one dear to the student's creed, one for daily life, and one for official use, creates a problem which is very difficult to overcome.

*(From **UNESCO Courier**, August 1983; article by Abdulaziz El Khoussy)*

# 4 Language study

### a) Vocabulary: growth and finance

Two recurring themes in the text concern growth and finance. Place the words from the text in the following list in the appropriate box:

*multiply / back / develop / promote / increase / expand / maintain / sponsor / flourish / support*

| Growth | Finance |
|--------|---------|
|        |         |

### b) Useful words and phrases

The following words are all used in the passage in comon phrases. Fit them into the new sentences given below:

*currently / letter / pace / gap / torn / inundated / arisen*

1 The _____ between the industrialised nations and the Third World is increasing.
2 We have been _____ with enquiries since the announcement.
3 He obeyed the instructions to the _____.
4 I am _____ between going with him and waiting here.
5 I am _____ working on a new experiment.
6 Some technical difficulties have _____ which will delay the project.
7 Since he could not keep up, he walked on at his own _____.

### c) Language focus: passive forms

The passive is often avoided in everyday speech in English. But in more serious or technical writing it occurs more frequently. There are at least fifteen examples of the passive in various forms in the above text. How many of them can you spot? What word, or phrase, if any, is the subject of the verb?

The following table sets out most of the forms of the passive. Use them as a reference for doing the exercise that follows:

| Active | Passive |
|--------|---------|
| to do | to be done |
| to have done | to have been done |
| doing | being done |
| does | is done |
| is/are doing | is/are being done |
| did | was done |
| was/were doing | was/were being done |
| has done | has been done |
| will do | will be done |
| will have done | will have been done |

**Note:** To derive the passive form of the verb from the active, replace the lexical part of the verb with the equivalent form of the verb 'to be' and add the past participle of the lexical form. The passive form will always have one more element than the active form.

**d) Activity**

Rewrite the following sentences in the passive. Omit the agent unless required. Which sentence sounds more formal? The first one has been done for you.

1 Some teachers teach a lot of nonsense in the classroom.
  A lot of nonsense is taught in the classroom

2 According to our history teacher, the Normans invaded England in 1066.

3 They have never satisfactorily explained the mystery of creation.

4 In the physics lesson, we placed the test-tube in a centrifuge.

5 They have awarded the best pupil a scholarship.

6 They gave him a last chance before expelling him.

7 The school is admitting a large number of new pupils this year.

8 We should see children and not hear them.

9 They have told us that Galileo invented the telescope.

10 I don't enjoy people beating me at sport in school.

11 They made him stay behind after class.

12 I will inform you of the result of your exam by letter.

# 5 Transfer

**a) Text**

Look at the picture below and write a sentence for each of the letters on the diagram describing what the people are doing.

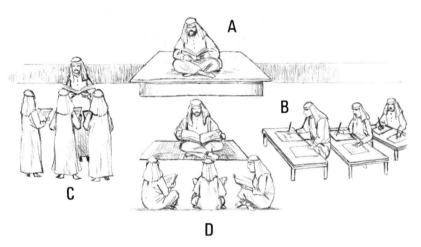

**b) Discussion**

How much time is or was spent in your school on religion? Do you think your government schools spend enough time on religion? How important do you think religion is in education?

# 6 Writing

**Write about one of these:**

  a) Describe the teacher who had most influence on you at school.
  b) Students should be allowed to choose which subjects they wish to study.

# MODULE 3
## EDUCATION C

## 1 Setting the scene

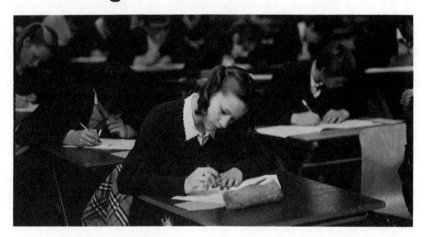

## 2 Vocabulary

| | |
|---|---|
| make the break /meɪk ðə ˈbreɪk/ | start something new |
| 'A' levels /ˈeɪ levəlz/ | school exam in individual subjects taken at 17/18 |
| on the dole /on ðə ˈdəul/ | receiving government money when out of work |
| BSc /bɪ es ˈsɪ/ | Bachelor of Science (university degree in science) |
| grant /grɑːnt/ | government money for studying |
| go on about /gəu ˈon əbaut/ | complain about |
| catering /ˈkeɪtərɪŋ/ | providing food |
| sandwich course /ˈsænwɪtʃ kɔːs/ | course of study between periods of practical work |
| clerical /ˈklerɪkl/ | to do with the office |
| better off /ˈbetər of/ | in a better position |

## 3 Tape

On the tape, a girl is explaining her decision to leave school to a family friend. As you listen, answer the following questions:

a) How do her parents feel about her leaving school?
b) How do her teachers feel?
c) How does the family friend feel?

## 4 Language study

**a) Vocabulary and pronunciation: marked and unmarked forms**

'waitress, manageress': In English, there are often two forms of a noun where it refers to males or females. Historically, the male form (often ending in '-er' or '- man') is usually the unmarked form, that is to say we use it to refer to the person or animal when we are not specifying the gender. However, with the improvement in sexual equality (at least for human beings!), there is a trend towards new undifferentiated forms. For example, the word 'chairperson' is steadily replacing 'chairman' where the sexual distinction is not important.

Fill in the gaps in the following table and underline the stressed syllable in the longer words:

39

| Unmarked | Male | Female |
|---|---|---|
| person | | |
| — | steward | |
| police officer | | |
| — | scout | |
| model | | |
| — | mayor | |
| — | | actress |
| nurse | | |
| spouse | | |
| parents-in-law | | |
| dog | | |
| cat | | |
| | ram | |
| pig | | |
| cattle | | |
| | | mare |
| deer | | |
| | cock | |
| duck | | |
| goose | | |

**b) Useful words and phrases: 'make' v. 'do'**
'make a mistake, do well': The choice of 'make' or 'do' often causes problems for learners of English. There have been several suggestions to try to help categorise the distinction, (eg 'do' = 'act', 'make' = 'construct') but it's basically a matter of learning through experience. Complete the following sentences with an appropriate form of 'make' or 'do'.

1  Have you _____ your homework?
2  I hate _____ the housework.
3  Drink this: it'll _____ you good.
4  Take this: it'll _____ you better.
5  Could you _____ me a favour?
6  I could _____ with a bit of help.
7  You'll just have to _____ without.
8  Please don't _____ fun of me.
9  He refuses to _____ business with me.
10  Don't forget to _____ your bed.
11  He insists on _____ the journey alone.
12  Just _____ your job and stop complaining.

**c) Language focus: present tense with future reference**
The girl talks about her future using a number of *time* (when, once) or *conditional I* (if) clauses. Note that the tense in these subordinate clauses is always present (simple, continuous or perfect). The only apparent exception is in a Conditional I where 'will' is used in the meaning of 'insist on' (positive) or 'refuse' (negative) — eg 'If you will keep talking, I shall leave' or 'If you won't help, I shall do it myself.'

**d) Activity**
Rewrite the sentences overleaf using each of the following subordinating conjunctions once only:

*when / whenever / if / as / before / until / while / as soon as / once / the moment*

eg   *He's going to take up archery on his retirement.*
    *He's going to take up archery when he retires.*

1   On arrival, he will go straight to his hotel.

2   He may resign and we will lose his services.

3   Having reached the summit, you will have a magnificent view.

4   Elaine will only graduate at the age of 25.

5   Simon is going to go to Edinburgh on his next visit to Scotland.

6   During the walk, you will notice a wide variety of birds.

7   They will start to build immediately on receiving permission.

8   The expedition will send back daily reports during the climb.

9   He will be drunk before the end of the party.

10   Our representative will send us details of every sale.

## 5   Transfer

### a)   Tape

Make up questions to which the following are answers from the tape:

1   _____ ?   Sixteen.

2   _____ ?   Over a year.

3   _____ ?   Fifteen.

4   _____ ?   He was quite upset.

5   _____ ?   Three years.

6   _____ ?   Because her parents work.

7   _____ ?   He's still out of work.

8   _____ ?   To the Technical College.

9   _____ ?   Mr Easton.

10   _____ ?   More practical.

### b)   Discussion

What percentage of children go to university in your country?
Some parents and children feel that university is a waste of time. Do you agree?
Should the government provide grants to enable any student who wishes to, to go to university?

## 6   Writing

**Write about one of these:**
a)   Describe how the average person in your country pays for university education.
b)   Write a letter to a rich relative asking him or her to support you at university.

## 1 Setting the scene

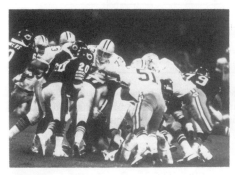

## 2 Vocabulary

| | |
|---|---|
| background: /ˈbækgraund/ | past experience |
| bright /braɪt/ | intelligent |
| eventually /ɪˈventʃuəlɪ/ | finally, in the end |
| stuck with /ˈstʌk wɪð/ | unable to escape from |
| swap /swop/ | change |
| cut out for /kʌt ˈaut fɔ:/ | suitable for |
| postgraduate /pəustˈgrædjuət/ | higher degree level |
| abstruse /æbˈstrus/ | difficult to understand |
| switch /swɪtʃ/ | change |
| retire /rɪˈtaɪə/ | stop work in old age |

## 3 Tape

On the tape you will hear a discussion between two people about the value of higher education. While listening to the them, find the answers to the following questions:

a) At what age do English children start to specialise?
b) In what way does John think the American university system is better?
c) How has the job situation changed since the speakers were younger?

## 4 Language study

**a) Vocabulary and pronunciation**

Fill in the following table of word families from words used by the speakers and underline the stressed syllable for each word:

| Adjective | Verb | Concept | Person |
|-----------|------|---------|--------|
| educational | educate | education | educator |
| special | | | — |
| physical | — | | |
| scientific | — | | |
| acceptable | | | — |
| practical | | | |
| flexible | | | — |
| technical | — | | |

**b) Useful words and phrases: common metaphors**
John uses two quite common metaphors to explain the problems of university students — 'You've burnt your bridges', 'You can't change horses in mid-stream'. Do you know what they mean? Here they are, together with some others. Link them correctly.

| | | | |
|---|---|---|---|
| 1 | burn your bridges | a) | obey orders |
| 2 | change horses in mid-stream | b) | a difficult situation |
| 3 | water under the bridge | c) | very different |
| 4 | spill the beans | d) | destroy your alternatives |
| 5 | jump the gun | e) | something past which will not return |
| 6 | toe the line | f) | a person who spoils other people's pleasure |
| 7 | hand it to somebody | g) | start too quickly |
| 8 | a dog in a manger | h) | reveal a secret |
| 9 | a far cry | i) | change activities |
| 10 | a sticky wicket | j) | congratulate someone |

**c) Language focus: 'some', 'any' and 'no' compounds**
The standard rule here is that 'some' and its compounds are used with positive sentences, while 'any' and its compounds are used with interrogatives and negatives and 'no' compounds are always negative, as in the table below:

| Positive | Interrogative | Negative | | |
|----------|---------------|----------|---|---|
| some + noun | any + noun | negative | any --- | no --- |
| some | any | verb or | any | none |
| someone | anyone | verb + | + anyone | no-one |
| somebody | anybody | *negative | anybody | nobody |
| something | anything | adverb | anything | nothing |
| somewhere | anywhere | | anywhere | nowhere |

* Negative adverbs include: rarely, never, scarcely, hardly

The problem area often lies with the interrogatives, because 'some' and its compounds can be used where the questioner hopes for the answer 'yes'.
eg 'Can somebody give me a hand?' or 'Would you like some tea?'
Also note that we often use 'them/their' for co-reference instead of 'him or her', eg 'If anybody calls, tell them I'm out'.

**d) Activity**
Fill in the gaps in the following:
1 Have _____ of the guests arrived? — No, _____ of them as yet.
2 _____ is missing. Has _____ left? — No, _____'s left — we're all still here.
3 I put my glasses down _____, and now I can't find them _____. Has _____ seen them?

4 Would you like _____ advice? Don't tell _____ about it until you are sure.

5 I'm sorry, it's me again. Were you expecting _____ else?

6 _____ tells me you're angry. I hope it isn't _____ I've said.

7 Arthur probably helped more than _____ to solve the problem.

8 _____ fool could tell you that!

9 Let's bury it _____ in the garden. — But what if _____ finds it?

10 No, you can't borrow _____ more. I've got _____ money left. Why don't you ask _____ else for a change?

# 5  Transfer

### a)  Tape

Listen to the tape again and answer the following:

### Section I

1 John feels that
a) education is important for bright people.
b) people must be bright to have an education.
c) education doesn't really matter for bright people.
d) all bright people should have an education.

2 When do children start to specialise in English schools?
a) In their second year.     b) At about 14.
c) At about 13.     d) After 'A' levels.

3 John claims that for 'A' level you cannot study
a) French and German.     b) History and Geography.
c) Chemistry and Biology.     d) Physics and English.

### Section II

True or false, according to the speakers?
1 Most children have not decided what they want to do by the age of 16.
2 University students must take a wide range of subjects.
3 You can easily change subjects at a British university.

### Section III

Fill in the gaps:
1 John claims that American students can choose their subjects _____ certain limits.
2 Peter feels that American students don't have the _____ of knowledge they should have.
3 He feels that John is _____ the amount of pure learning needed.

### b)  Discussion

How free are you to choose the subjects you study at school or university? How useful are these subjects in preparing you for a job?

# 6  Writing

### Write about one of these:

a) A university education is a waste of time for most people.
b) Compare your university system with that of America and Britain.

# MODULE 4
## RELIGION A

## 1 Setting the scene

## 2 Vocabulary

worship *n* (l.1)    religious activities, especially attending church
observance *n* (l.2)    activities in accordance with religious belief
adherent *n* (l.6)    follower
mutual *adj* (l.17)    equally shared by each
uphold *vt* (l.20)    support
ordain *vt* (l.31)    make someone a priest or religious leader
evangelism *n* (l.57)    preaching Christianity
extinct *adj* (l.63)    no longer existing

## 3 Text

While reading the text, find the answers to the following questions:
a) What are the two established churches in Britain?
b) To which church must the Sovereign belong?
c) What are the four major Free Churches?

# ■ THE CHRISTIAN CHURCHES IN BRITAIN

Everyone in Britain has the right of religious freedom (in teaching, worship and observance) without interference from the community or the State. There are two established churches, that is, churches legally recognised as official churches of the State: in England the (Anglican) Church of England, and
5  in Scotland the (Presbyterian) Church of Scotland. There is no precise information about the number of church adherents since no inquiries are normally made about religious beliefs in censuses or other official returns, and each church adopts its own criteria in counting its members.

About one-sixth of the adult population in Britain are members of a Christian
10  church and there are considerable regional variations in church membership: England has the lowest membership with 13 per cent, Wales has 23 per cent, Scotland 37 per cent, and Northern Ireland the highest with 80 per cent. There has been a decline in recent years in both the number of full-time ministers and the recorded adult membership of the larger Christian denominations. This has
15  been accompanied by a significant growth among small break-away, independent, or Pentecostal churches and new religious movements.

The Church of England's relationship with the State is one of mutual obligation — privileges accorded to the Church balanced by certain duties which it must fulfil. The Sovereign must always be a member of the Church, and pro-
20  mises to uphold it: Church of England archbishops, bishops and deans are appointed by the Sovereign on the advice of the Prime Minister: all clergy take an oath of allegiance to the Crown.

The Church has two provinces: in Canterbury, comprising 30 dioceses, and York, 14 dioceses. The Archbishop of Canterbury is 'Primate of All England', and
25  the Archbishop of York 'Primate of England'. The dioceses are divided into 13,500 parishes. Attendances at services on a normal Sunday are around 1.2 million. Many people who rarely, if ever, attend services, nevertheless regard themselves as belonging to the Church of England (amounting perhaps to some 60 per cent of the population). At present, men only are admitted to the
30  priesthood, but in 1984 the General Synod voted in favour of legislation being prepared to enable women to be ordained priests: final decisions on the matter, however, are not expected to be taken for some years.

The Anglican Communion comprising provinces in Britain and overseas has a total membership of about 70 million. In the British Isles, there are four pro-
35  vinces: The Church of England (established), the Church of Wales, the Scottish Episcopal Church in Scotland, and the Church of Ireland.

The Church of Scotland has a presbyterian form of government, that is, government by elders. It is the national church of Scotland, and comprises 1765 churches. Both men and women are admitted to the ministry.
40  The expression 'Free Churches' is commonly used to describe those Protestant churches in Britain which, unlike the Church of England and the Church of Scotland, are not established. In the course of history they have developed their own convictions in church order and worship. All the major Free Churches — Methodist, Baptist, United Reformed and Salvation Army — admit both men and
45  women to the ministry. The Methodist Church, the largest of the Free Churches with nearly 500,000 adult full members, originated in the eighteenth century following the evangelical revival under John Wesley.

The Baptists are nearly all grouped in associations of churches, with a total membership of about 166,600. In addition, there are separate Baptist Unions for
50  Scotland, Wales and Ireland and other Baptist Churches. The United Reformed Church, with some 140,000 members, was formed in 1972 when the Congregational Church in England and Wales (the oldest community of dissenters in Britain) and the Presbyterian Church of England merged. In 1981 there was a further union with the Reformed Association of the Churches of Christ. The
55  Salvation Army, founded in Britain in 1865, has since spread to 85 other countries. Within Britain there are 60,000 active members operating from nearly 1000 centres of worship. The Salvation Army's distinctive ministry of Christian evangelism and practical care is also expressed through the work of 170 social service centres, ranging from hostels for the homeless to homes for the elderly,
60  for abused children and for teenagers on probation, and recreational centres for Service personnel.

The Roman Catholic hierarchy in England and Wales, which became temporarily extinct during the sixteenth century, was restored in 1850: the Scottish hierarchy became extinct in the early seventeenth century and was restored in
65 1878. It is estimated that there are some 5.7 million adherents to the Roman Catholic faith in Britain. Men only are admitted to the priesthood. In 1982 Pope John Paul II paid a pastoral visit to Britain, the first by a reigning pontiff.

*(From Britain 1986 Handbook)*

# 4   Language study

### a)   Vocabulary: church hierarchy and organisation

The text mentions a number of church offices and organisational areas.
Grade the church offices marked + in descending hierarchical order.
Grade the organisational areas marked * in descending hierarchical order.
The first one has been done for you.

| | | |
|---|---|---|
| ministers | +archbishop (   ) | *province (1) |
| ministry | +bishop (   ) | *diocese (   ) |
| clergy | +dean (   ) | *parish (   ) |
| priests | +primate (1) | |
| priesthood | | |

### b)   Useful words and phrases: freedom and obligation

First, check that you understand the following words from the text. Then mark those words below which refer to 'freedom' with an 'F', and those which refer to 'obligation' with an 'O'.

right
freedom
obligation
privilege
duty

### c)   Language focus: nouns and their classification

Look at the following subclassification of nouns

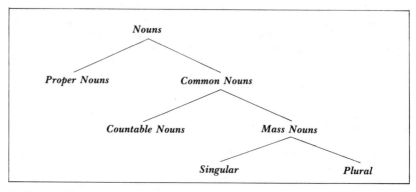

### 1   Proper Nouns

Normally these do not take the article ('the' or 'a'), eg Britain, England, Canterbury.
In exceptional cases they do take 'the', eg the Church of England, the State, the Sovereign, the Crown, but this article cannot be replaced by a demonstrative determiner ('this', 'that', 'these', 'those').

### 2   Common Nouns

These can be divided into *countable* and *mass*:
a)   Countable
These are grammatically distinguishable from proper nouns and mass nouns in that they have a singular/plural contrast, eg member/members
b)   Mass
These are nouns which have no number contrast.
They can be divided into *singular* and *plural*

i) Singular words which have no plural form
eg information, advice, interference, legislation, worship.

ii) Plural words which have no singular form
eg clergy, people.

**NB** In certain cases plural mass common nouns and singular countable common nouns which refer to 'more than one' can take either a singular or a plural verb, The singular is used if the noun is regarded as a single body; the plural if the noun is regarded as a group of individuals, eg:

eg The clergy *is* expected to take an oath of allegiance.
The clergy *are* expected to vote in favour.

The committee *has* come to a decision.
The committee *have* gone home.

### d) Activity

1 Look at the sentences below.
Then indicate in the space provided whether the sentence is grammatically correct (√) or incorrect (✗):

a) The government have decided to investigate the matter further. ( )
b) This news is of great interest to us all. ( )
c) But we expect a Sovereign to uphold the Church. ( )
d) All our advices have been ignored. ( )
e) The State must decide on matters of national interest. ( )
f) A clergy visits his parishioners regularly. ( )

2 Now complete the following text using the words given below:

*right / freedom / privilege / duty / responsibility / law*

Use each word only once.

Is (a)_____ of speech a (b)_____ or a (c)_____? If the (d)_____ gives us this freedom, do we have any (e)_____ for what we say? In any society can there be right without (f)_____ or privilege without responsibility?

## 5 Transfer

### a) Text
Refer to the text and then complete the following table.

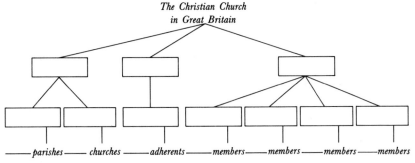

*The Christian Church
in Great Britain*

——parishes—— churches ——adherents—— members——members ——members ——members

### b) Discussion
Compare the variety of religious movements in the UK with the situation in your country.

## 6 Writing

**Write about one of these:**
a) Describe the main religious movements in your country.
b) Some form of religious education in school is desirable. What form should this education take?

# MODULE 4
## RELIGION B

## 1 Setting the scene

## 2 Vocabulary

| | | |
|---|---|---|
| grove | *n* (l.8) | group of trees |
| barber | *n* (l.15) | men's hairdresser |
| craft | *n* (l.17) | job or trade needing skill, especially with one's hands |
| incarnation | *n* (l.20) | physical form on earth of a god |
| deity | *n* (l.24) | god |
| epidemic | *n* (l.34) | disease that spreads rapidly |
| fate | *n* (l.37) | force, beyond human control, that is believed to decide events |
| dwarf | *n* (l.38) | very small man |
| compatibility | *n* (l.44) | suitability for each other |
| dowry | *n* (l.44) | property or money that a woman brings to her husband on marriage |
| tension | *n* (l.51) | feeling of nervous anxiety between people of different religions |

## 3 Text

While reading the text, find the answers to the following questions:
a)  How many main castes are there in Hinduism?
b)  How many local deities has Nanpur got?
c)  Who arranges a couple's marriage?

# ■ A VILLAGE CALLED NANPUR

The name of my village is Nanpur, which is one of India's 500,000 villages. It stands on the bank of the river Birupa in the Cuttack district of Orissa. It is part of a group of villages with a central market place at Balichandrapur, three kilometres away, where there is now a bank, a police station and a
5 post office. The village is connected by road with Cuttack, 48 kilometres south-west, the commercial centre of the State.

Nanpur has a population of about 3000 living in six settlements separated by mango groves and paddy fields. Each settlement is inhabited by one particular caste. Religious caste is the most important feature. It defines a person's place in
10 the village and the work he is expected to do. One is born into a caste and it cannot be changed.

Traditionally there are four castes — Brahmins, the priests; Kshatriyas, the warriors; Vaishyas, the businessmen; and Sudras, the servant caste. But over the years there have been many sub-castes relating to professions. There are
15 Brahmins, Karans — the administrators — farmers, barbers, astrologers and Harijans, formerly called Untouchables. The villagers are mainly farmers and craftsmen. Each craft is the property of a particular caste and together they form the village community.

The villagers of Nanpur are Hindus. They are religious. They believe in God
20 and his many incarnations. For them He is everywhere — in a man, in a tree, in a stone. According to Arjun Satpathi, the village Brahmin, God is light and energy, like the electric current. To him there is no difference between the gods of the Hindus, Muslims and Christians. Only the names are different.

Every village has a local deity. In Nanpur it is a piece of stone in the shape of
25 a shiva lingam — the male sexual organ, which is the symbol of the god Shiva. He is called Mahlia Buddha. He sits under the ancient varuna tree protecting the village. Kanhai Barik, the village barber, is the attendant to the deity. Kanhai, before starting his daily work, washes the deity, decorates it with vermilion and flowers, and offers food which has been given by the villagers. Clay animals are
30 presented. It is believed that the deity rides them during the night and goes from place to place guarding the village. Mahlia Buddha was donated to the village by the barber's great-great-great-grandmother, so only his family has the right to attend to the deity. In the old days Mahlia Buddha had a special power to cure smallpox and cholera. Now, although modern medicines have brought the epide-
35 mics under control, the power of the deity has not diminished. People believe in him and worship him for everything, even for modern medicines to be effective.

People believe in karma (fate) and the cycle of rebirth. This helps them to accept their situation. Padan is the only dwarf in the village and is popular, despite his disability. He is twenty-seven and runs a tea stall in the market place.
40 He recently married another dwarf from a distant village. Padan believes he is a dwarf in this life because of his actions in a previous incarnation.

Marriages are arranged by parents and the bride and bridegroom must belong to the same caste. The horoscopes are shown to the astrologer, who draws diagrams and forecasts their compatibility. The girl's father has to give a dowry,
45 although it is forbidden by law. The bride must be a virgin.

The women in Nanpur worship Satyapir, a Hindu-Muslim God, to bless them with sons. 'Satya' is the Hindu part meaning 'truth', and 'pir' in Islam means 'prophet'. It was a deliberate attempt to bring the two communities together through religion. There is a large Muslim settlement three kilometres from
50 Nanpur, and in a village on the other side of the river a single Muslim family lives surrounded by Brahmins. In spite of Hindu-Muslim tensions in other parts of India, the atmosphere around the village has remained peaceful.

There is great respect for education. Children start going to school at the age of four. The school starts with a prayer which acknowledges the presence of God
55 in nature. The children sing, 'Why should I be afraid of telling the truth? Even if I have to die, I must tell the truth. O God, please teach me this. I need nothing else.'

*(From* **UNESCO Courier,** *June 1983; article by P Mohanti)*

# 4 Language

## a) Vocabulary: communities

The following words are used in the text to describe communities according to the number of people living in the unit. Grade them in ascending order of size. The first one has been done for you.

village ( )
district ( )
settlement ( )
family ( )
parents (1)

The text also mentions a number of professions. Match the profession on the left with the description on the right.

| Profession | | Description | |
|---|---|---|---|
| 1 | priest | a) | soldier |
| 2 | warrior | b) | forecaster of events by reference to the sun, moon, stars and planets |
| 3 | servant | c) | men's hairdresser |
| 4 | astrologer | d) | religious leader |
| 5 | barber | e) | a person who works in a household for wages and/or accommodation |

## b) Useful words and phrases: 'only' and 'even'

'Only' is an adverb and an adjective. In both cases it has a restrictive meaning, eg .... so only his family has the right to attend to the deity. (nobody else except them)
Only the names are different. (nothing else except the names)
Padan is the only dwarf in the village ... (no other dwarf except him)
As an adverb, 'only' typically stands before the sentence element it focuses on; as an adjective 'only' stands before the noun it modifies.
(NB 'Only' cannot be used predicatively.)
'Even' is an adverb. It has a concessive and additive meaning, in other words it focuses on unexpected additional information,
eg People worship him for everything, even for modern medicines to be effective. (they worship him for that, too, unexpected as it is)
Even if I have to die, I must tell the truth. (unexpected as it is, I am prepared to die if I don't tell the truth)
Like 'only', 'even' typically stands before the sentence element it focuses on.

Now complete the following extract from a letter using 'only' or 'even' in the spaces given.

'... So John was clearly the (1)_____ person who could possibly pull it off by himself. But, in fact, on the day not (2)_____ he succeeded. So, we sat there thinking what to do next. Of course! There was Peter. We (3)_____ had to ask him. He'd be sure to help. Anyway, to cut a long story short, everyone was most impressed with the results, (4)_____ the MacKenzies. So, you see, I (5)_____ had to ask two people to get what I wanted. (6)_____ you must admit that's pretty good going.'

## c) Language focus: relative clauses

Relative clauses consist of two types — defining and non-defining. Defining relative clauses (also called restrictive relative clauses) provide essential information which restricts or clarifies the meaning of the preceding noun or noun phrase by specifying its meaning more exactly,
eg The school starts with a prayer which acknowledges the presence of God in nature.
Kanhai ... offers food which has been given by the villagers.
   Non-defining (or non-restrictive) relative clauses provide additional, non-essential, information,
eg The name of my village is Nanpur, which is one of India's 500,000 villages.

The horoscopes are shown to the astrologer, who draws diagrams ...

The two types of relative clauses can also be distinguished by the punctuation used. Non-defining clauses are enclosed by commas; defining clauses are not.

| | Defining & Non-defining | | Defining only |
| | Personal | Non-personal | Personal and non-personal |
|---|---|---|---|
| subjective | who | which | that |
| objective | who (m) | which | that, zero (no pronoun) |
| genitive | whose | of which/whose | |
| locative | | where | |
| temporal | | when | |

**d) Activity**

Combine the following pairs of sentences by using a relative clause in the correct position and adding appropriate punctuation where needed.
1  The Hindu religion has many deities. Most Indians belong to it.
2  Nearly every village in India has its own god. The inhabitants worship its personification.
3  Benares is the holy city of the Hindus. It is in the north of India.
4  Benares is the holy city of the Hindus. Many pilgrims visit it.
5  Holy men sit in the streets. The pilgrims visit them.
6  These holy men offer blessings. They are dressed in saffron robes.
7  The river is called the Ganges. It flows through the city.
8  Many Hindus visit Benares in their extreme old age. They are about to die then.
9  Every day there are funeral pyres on the banks of the Ganges. The corpses are burnt there.
10  The ashes are ceremoniously thrown into the river. They have been collected from the pyres.

# 5  Transfer

**a)  Text**

Now fill in the details in the table below.

| Profile of Nanpur |
|---|
| Population: _____ |
| District: _____ |
| State: _____ |
| Religion: _____ |
| Main castes: _____ |
| _____ |
| _____ |
| _____ |
| Village god: _____ |
| God worshipped by Nanpur women: _____ |

**b)  Discussion**

Religious caste or social class: Does every society need a way of labelling people according to religious or social criteria? What is the situation in your country?

# 6  Writing

**Write about one of these:**
a)  Write a letter to a foreign friend describing a religious festival.
b)  Religious festivals are becoming over-commercialised.

# MODULE 4
## RELIGION C

## 1 Setting the scene

## 2 Vocabulary

| | |
|---|---|
| dominate /ˈdɒmineɪt/ | have the most important place in |
| consideration /kənsɪdəˈreɪʃən/ | matter to be considered |
| peripheral /pəˈrɪfərəl/ | of small importance |
| conclude /kənˈkluːd/ | come to believe |
| collapse /kəˈlæps/ | breakdown |
| abandonment /əˈbændənmənt/ | giving up |
| notion /ˈnəʊʃən/ | idea |
| rational /ˈræʃənəl/ | based on reason |
| particle /ˈpɑːtɪkəl/ | very small piece of matter |
| ultimate /ˈʌltimət/ | final |

## 3 Tape

This listening text deals with religious belief in the UK. The Reverend James Boyd talks first about the change in the role of the Church over the last hundred years, and then goes on to examine the results of a recent survey into religious belief. While you are listening to the tape, find the answers to the following questions:

a) What type of thinking has replaced religious ideas?
b) What did the research team study?
c) Do the results of the survey indicate that Britain is a godless society?

# 4 Language study

## a) Vocabulary and pronunciation: religion and belief

The following list of words taken from the tape deals with the area of religion and belief. First, underline the syllable which carries the word stress. Then match the words on the left with the definitions on the right.
The first one is 1 spiritual and g).

| | | | |
|---|---|---|---|
| 1 | spiritual | a) | the ability to look into the future |
| 2 | doctrine | b) | belief in many gods |
| 3 | fate | c) | the ability to see events not clearly visible |
| 4 | paganism | d) | not explained by natural laws |
| 5 | superstition | e) | religious principle |
| 6 | premonition | f) | cause beyond human control which decides events |
| 7 | clairvoyance | g) | non-material |
| 8 | supernatural | h) | belief not based on reason or fact |

## b) Useful words and phrases: phrasal verbs with 'look'

First, complete the verb phrases below, which have been taken from the text, by selecting an appropriate particle (adverb or preposition), so that each verb phrase has the same meaning as the words given:

| | |
|---|---|
| 1 to look _____ | to take care of |
| 2 to look _____ | to examine |
| 3 to look _____ | to depend on |
| 4 to look _____ | to consider |

Now complete the following expressions using one of the above verb phrases with 'look' in each sentence:
5  It's no use _____ your crystal ball.
6  God _____ those who _____ themselves.
7  I can't understand your point of view. Just _____ the importance of religion as a world force.
8  Priests have traditionally held an important position in society, and we have always _____ them in times of trouble.

## c) Language focus: quantifiers and adverbs of degree

The following table deals with the notion of scale of amount. On the left are the quantifiers (determiners or pronouns) which express the main points on the scale; on the right are the adverbs which indicate corresponding notions in the area of degree.

| quantifiers | adverbs of degree |
|---|---|
| all | entirely/totally/absolutely/fully/completely |
| most | mostly |
| many/much | very/(very) much/enormously/greatly |
| some | quite/rather/somewhat |
| a few/a little | a little/a bit |
| few/little | scarcely/hardly |
| no | not ... at all |

Now look at the following sentences taken from the tape exemplifying the use of adverbs of degree.
— scientific and rational thinking determines *entirely* ...
— .... by forces *totally* outside our scientific or rational understanding

— this view has been *very* influential
— religious beliefs matter *enormously* to them

— church attendance has gone down *quite* markedly
— it seems a *rather* peripheral thing

— they supported only *a little* important Christian ideas about God

— religious ideas are *hardly* relevant . . .
— they have *scarcely* any value . . .

— religion does*n't* fit into it *at all*

**d) Activity**

Select the appropriate quantifier or adverb of degree:

(1) _____ (Most/Most of) religions accept the widely-held belief in one god. In addition, (2) _____ (much/many) religions share (3) _____ (quite/somewhat) a similar set of practices; and historically (4) _____ (no/scarcely) society has emerged which didn't have any religion (5) _____ (hardly/at all). And although in many countries of the Western world, religious practice is declining, (6) _____ (all/most) these countries (7) _____ (fully/all) accept the importance of religious freedom. We can (8) _____ (little/hardly) imagine a society in which (9) _____ (some/few) of man's greatest monuments are turned into museums.

# 5 Transfer

**a) Tape**

Complete the following table:

| Results of the survey into religious belief in the UK | | |
|---|---|---|
| | Percentage of responses | |
| | Yes | No./ Don't know |
| Belief in ultimate spiritual power | | |
| Belief that Jesus was God's son | | |
| Acceptance of major Christian principles | | |
| Belief in fate | | |
| Belief in luck | | |
| Belief in premonition | | |
| Belief in clairvoyance | | |

**b) Discussion**

As more and more of the 'wonders of the universe' are explained in scientific and rational terms, is the role of religion bound to diminish?

# 6 Writing

**Write about one of these:**

a) Write a letter to a public official complaining about the policy of encouraging tourists to visit religious sites.
b) How do you view the future of religion?

## 1   Setting the scene

## 2   Vocabulary

| | |
|---|---|
| globe /gləub/ | earth |
| recite /rɪˈsaɪt/ | say aloud from memory |
| creed /kriːd/ | declaration of religious belief |
| apostle /əˈposəl/ | one chosen by God to spread his message |
| set /set/ | fixed |
| alms /ɑːmz/ | collection of money to be given to the poor |
| fast /fɑːst/ | going without food |
| pilgrimage /ˈpɪlgrəmɪdʒ/ | sacred journey |
| ritual /ˈrɪtʃuəl/ | for religious purposes |
| purity /ˈpjuərətɪ/ | religious cleanliness |

## 3   Tape

This listening text deals with the religious practices of Islam. On the tape a Muslim explains the most important religious observances required of Muslims. While you are listening to the tape, find the answers to the following questions:

a)   How many practices must every believing Muslim carry out?
b)   How long does Ramadan last?
c)   What is the first action of a pilgrim visiting Mecca?

## 4   Language study

**a)   Vocabulary and pronunciation: abstract and animate nouns**

The table below is divided into abstract nouns and animate nouns. First complete the table. Then underline the syllable which carries the word stress.

| Abstract noun | Animate noun |
|---|---|
| following | follower |
| | believer |
| | the faithful |
| devotion | |
| | guide |
| | the pure |
| | the poor |
| | brother |

### b) Useful words and phrases: times of the day

The tape introduces a number of words describing times of the day. Organise them in chronological order. The first one has been done for you.

     dawn (1)

     dusk ( )

     sunrise ( )

     noon ( )

     sunset ( )

### c) Language focus: obligation and prohibition

The table below deals with the notions of *obligation* and *prohibition*. It categorises verb phrases as follows:

obligation to do something

obligation not to do something, ie prohibition

no obligation

| Obligation to do something | Obligation not to do something | No obligation |
|---|---|---|
| must<br>have to<br>need to<br>be required to<br>be supposed to<br>be obliged to | mustn't<br>not be allowed to<br>be prohibited from | needn't<br>not have to |

### d) Activity

Rewrite the following sentences using the verb phrase given in brackets.

The first sentence has been done for you.

1  Every religion requires its followers to observe certain practices. (must)

    The followers of every religion <u>must observe certain practices.</u>

2  On the one hand religions prescribe necessary behaviour for their followers during their worldly existence. (be supposed to)

    On the one hand religions prescribe how their followers ＿＿＿＿＿＿＿＿＿＿

＿＿＿＿＿＿＿＿＿＿＿＿＿＿＿＿＿＿＿＿＿＿＿＿＿＿＿＿＿＿＿＿＿＿＿

3  On the other hand most religions also lay down practices to be followed to achieve peace in the afterlife. (be required to)

    On the other hand most religions also lay down what practices ＿＿＿＿＿＿

4  In some religions there is a ban on certain types of food. (be prohibited)

    In some religions certain types of food ＿＿＿＿＿＿＿＿＿＿＿＿＿＿＿＿

5 For example in Islam and Judaism people mustn't eat pork. (not allowed to)
For example in Islam and Judaism people _____

6 Although in Islam there is a ban on alcohol (be prohibited), in Judaism there is no requirement for the people to abstain. (not have to)
Although in Islam alcohol _____, in Judaism the people _____.

7 The Catholic church accepts the weakness of the flesh and people's subsequent need to confess their sins. (have to)
The Catholic church accepts the weakness of the flesh and that people _____

_____.

8 Despite falling church attendance, especially in the western world, there is no need yet for religious leaders to worry about the disappearance of religion. (needn't)
Despite falling church attendance, especially in the western world, religious leaders _____.

Now complete this extract from a sermon by inserting each of the following words once:

*must / mustn't / needs to / don't need to / have to*

... So, my friends, obligations come both from inside and outside us. The external obligations one _(1)_____ fulfil to the best of one's abilities, and one _(2)_____ avoid one's responsibilities. As for internal obligations, we _(3)_____ lead our lives as our hearts would see fit. For finally each one of us _(4)_____ give a final account. And I _(5)_____ remind you that the day of reckoning will surely come. As I am your ...

# 5 Transfer

## a) Tape
Indicate in the table below the obligatory, prohibited and not obligatory practices of Islam.
Use the following symbols:

O+ = obligatory
O− = prohibited
−O = not obligatory

| | O+ | O− | −O |
|---|---|---|---|
| pray five times a day | | | |
| only pray in a mosque | | | |
| eat and drink during Ramadan | | | |
| make the pilgrimage to Mecca | | | |
| children observe the fast of Ramadan | | | |
| non-Muslims visit Mecca | | | |

## b) Discussion
Discuss the obligatory and prohibited practices in your country's religion(s).

# 6 Writing

## Write about one of these:
a) Describe the practices of your religion.
b) Religious dogma is a form of authoritarian control.

# MODULE 5
## GEOGRAPHY A

## 1 Setting the scene

## 2 Vocabulary

| | | |
|---|---|---|
| deceptive *adj* | (l.2) | giving a false impression |
| summit *n* | (l.3) | the top of a mountain |
| site *n* | (l.7) | place, location |
| scour *vt* | (l.12) | clean completely |
| pollen *n* | (l.15) | fine yellow dust on flowers |
| sediment *n* | (l.15) | mud, material carried by water |
| munch *vt* | (l.21) | eat |
| patch *n* | (l.23) | small area |
| imprint *n* | (l.35) | mark left on or in something |
| plunder *vi* | (l.39) | take goods/property by force in time of war |
| tackle *vt* | (l.57) | fight against |

## 3 Text

As you are reading the text, find the answers to the following questions:
a) Why are the Lake District mountains bare?
b) Who were the first people to live in the Lake District?
c) What was the main influence of the Scandinavian invaders?

# ■ THE LAKE DISTRICT

This piece of mountain scenery looks as if it is the work entirely of Nature in its most volcanic mood, and yet it is quite deceptive. These mountains were once wooded up to the summits, over 2000 feet, and the woodland was cleared by prehistoric man with a stone axe of a kind which has been found up on the Pike of Stickle. There was a tremendous trade in these axes; they have been found in Dorset, Wiltshire and Hampshire, and we call the sites where they were made 'axe factories'. The men of that time discovered in this great mass of rock an intrusive rock harder than all the rest. How they found it we do not know.

The Lake District, shaped and formed to a great extent during the last Ice Age, has seen numerous vegetational changes since the retreat of the glaciers. What was once a densely wooded landscape was scoured of vegetation, but the ice left behind enough surface soil for the high country to be recolonised: in other words, for the trees to come back. We know all this from identifying the pollen from trees found in the sediments of the lakes. We know exactly what sorts of trees grew and at what height. By Neolithic times, say 4000 to 5000 years ago, the mountains were wooded, and man was beginning to clear the forest from above.

But it was not only primitive man working with his axes and, probably, with fire, who opened up this landscape, creating clearings for his animals. The animals helped him; the sheep and goats, above all, munched every seedling that tried to grow again. Not much is left of the original woodland. Botanists, however, recognise what they call 'relict' woodland, patches of what the fells must have looked like originally. Miles of what are now bare fells were once heavily wooded.

Since the prehistoric axe trade developed very early on, you find ancient trade routes, now mere mountain tracks, most of them, crossing high passes. There is one broad path called High Street, not in the sense that we use it in modern towns, since the emphasis is on 'High' and it runs along the top of the peaks. These tracks have been in use since prehistoric times, and the modern fell walker still uses them. Near one of the 'axe factories', an axe was picked up which had been trodden on by fell walkers and scratched by them for years before anybody realised what it really was.

The Romans had no reason to interfere with the natives in the remote hills and dales, provided they gave no trouble, and thus they left very little imprint. Life went on at the farming level, but the next enemies came from across the sea, which can be seen gleaming on the horizon from Hard Knott. They came from the West, from Ireland, though in fact they were Norwegians. First they came to plunder, then they settled and became colonists. They not only took over the old settlements, they were also the first people to push into the heart of the mountains, up the valleys, to create new ones. Their imprint on the landscape, though exaggerated, I think, by the number of names of Norse origin, was very powerful indeed.

The name 'Watendlath' is pure Scandinavian, meaning 'the end of the water', which is a quite characteristic setting in the Lake District. Three or four farmsteads on a stream, grouped together, for security probably, and co-operation in farming and warmth. It is a hamlet rather than a village. The hamlet kind of settlement is really suited to a pastoral economy with a few cows and sheep on each farm, and probably, coming from Norway with a very similar topography, the Norsemen brought the hamlet with them. It could not expand into a village in such surroundings, when the countryside would support only a limited population no matter what was done to it. 'Thwaite' is the old Norse word for 'clearing'; in some places, the ground was so covered with glacial boulders that it gave its name to the whole settlement — hence, Stonethwaite. You get a very good idea of the primeval landscape from the great rock outcrops which show what kind of country the Norse colonists had to tackle.

Another very attractive feature of the landscape is the primitive-looking bowed bridge, a single arch over a small beck. One of the best is at 'Throstle-garth'. 'Throstle' means a thrush, 'garth' is the Scandinavian word for an

enclosure, and there the sheep were brought in from over the fells to be driven to the nearest market.

*(From **One Man's England** by WG Hoskins)*

# 4 Language study

### a) Vocabulary: dimension and size

The passage mentions several adjectives to describe size. What are their corresponding nouns and opposites?

| Adjective (How _____ is it?) | Noun (What _____ is it?) | Opposite adjective |
| --- | --- | --- |
| high | | |
| deep | | |
| broad | | |
| wide | | |
| long | | |
| big | | |
| large | | |

### b) Useful words and phrases: 'as' v. 'like'

'This piece of mountain scenery looks as if it is the work of nature ...'

'as if' can be followed either by the hypothetical past ('looks as if it were ...') or by the present, as here. The former sounds more formal. It is often confused with 'like', which, in this context, should be followed by a noun construction, eg 'This piece of mountain scenery looks like the work ...'.

'As' and 'like' are also often confused in sentences such as:

He is working as a teacher. (he is doing the job)

He is acting like a fool. (but he is not a fool)

Which do you use in these sentences?

1  He drives _____ a maniac.
2  What black clouds! It looks _____ rain.
3  You look _____ if you'd seen a ghost!
4  John works _____ a hotel porter in the holidays to earn money.
5  Nobody plays football _____ Maradona!

### c) Language focus: nominal clauses

The nominal clause introduced by a *Wh*-element can be:

subject, eg   What was once a densely wooded landscape was scoured of vegetation

direct object, eg   How they found it we do not know.

We know exactly what sort of trees grew and to what height.

prepositional complement, eg   Miles of what are now bare fells were once heavily wooded.

These should not be confused with other relative clauses, where the clause element is linked to a sentence element already expressed. Compare the following two sentences:

What the Vikings left behind was merely a few place-names. (Nominal)

All that the Vikings left behind was a few place-names. (Relative)

### d) Activity

Fill the gaps in the following sentences with an appropriate *Wh*-element or relative pronoun.

1  You should not believe all _____ historians say about the origins of these settlements.
2  Few books will tell you _____ you need to know.
3  Everything _____ is known today is based upon conjecture.
4  Although we know the precise location, there is no clear evidence about

exactly _____ or _____ the settlements were formed.

5  _____ were known as 'axe factories' were discovered in Dorset.

6  _____ they were transported to the Lake District at this time is not clear.

7  It has never been proved _____ the first people were to colonise the valleys.

8  From aerial photographs we know exactly _____ the settlements looked like.

9  And from _____ these settlements look like we can surmise something about the life style of the early inhabitants.

10  _____ the Romans never penetrated these valleys remains a mystery.

# 5  Transfer

### a)  Text

Fill in the gaps in the following text, and then refer to the text to check your choices:

The Lake District, (1)_____ and formed during the last (2)_____ Age, has seen many (3)_____ since the (4)_____ of the glaciers. The whole (5)_____ was scoured of vegetation but the ice left just enough (6)_____ soil (7)_____ the high country to be (8)_____; in other words, for the trees to come (9)_____. We know all this (10)_____ identifying the pollen from trees found in the (11)_____ of lakes. We know (12)_____ what sort of trees (13)_____ and to what (14)_____.

### b)  Discussion

The Lake District is a largely unspoilt area of natural beauty, which is now carefully protected as a National Park. Are there such areas in your country? How far should people go to preserve such areas and prevent development?

# 6  Writing

**Write about one of these:**

a)  Describe an area of outstanding natural beauty in your country.

b)  People are steadily destroying the environment.

# MODULE 5
## GEOGRAPHY B

## 1 Setting the scene

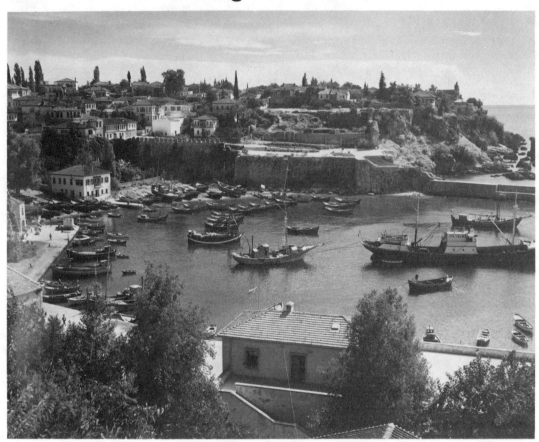

## 2 Vocabulary

| | | |
|---|---|---|
| polyglot *adj* | (l.7) | speaking many languages |
| random *adj* | (l.12) | without plan or direction |
| silt *vt* | (l.13) | fill with mud |
| pace *n* | (l.23) | speed |
| boast *vt* | (l.37) | possess with pride |
| limb *n* | (l.53) | leg |
| tributary *n* | (l.65) | smaller river joining a larger one |
| the fit *n pl* | (l.79) | people in good physical condition |
| breath-taking *adj* | (l.82) | exciting, beautiful |
| clad *adj* | (l.91) | covered |
| inkling *n* | (l.106) | idea |

## 3 Text

As you are reading the text, answer the following questions:
a) What does the writer find most interesting about the area?
b) How does he feel about crowds of tourists?
c) Does he prefer to travel around or stay in one centre?

# ■ TURKEY FOR THE TOURIST

From Izmir, halfway down the west coast, Kusadasi, some 88 kilometers to the south, is the obvious holidaymaker's centre. It has a marina capable of harbouring over 500 yachts, with boutiques, restaurants and polyglot nightlife, from which hotels and holiday villages have spread along the beautiful coast.

Here, the Maeander, the river that gave its name to the English language as the word for random wandering, has silted all the old cities and pushed a new coastline as much as 18 kilometres out into the Aegean since St Paul was there, with shallow beaches for mile upon mile to the south of Kusadasi: perfect for small children. Coach tours make it cheap and easy to visit the major classical sites, but it may make better sense to take a taxi early in the morning, beat the crowds and take things at your own pace. For a whole day trip, find the driver the night before, agree the price (he expects you to haggle), round it up with a tip, and always share your picnic with him.

Ephesus is within spitting distance — under 10 kilometres to the north east, and is a great Roman port now isolated from the sea by silt, where the young Alexander the Great was so impressed by the partially-completed Temple of Artemis and St Paul's teaching started a riot. Shattered by earthquakes, it now boasts one of the grandest Metro-Goldwyn-Mayer-type archaeological reconstructions — the Library of Celsus, a perfectly preserved and very public lavatory, temples, baths, brothels, splendid marble streets, and a stadium where you can easily imagine Ben Hur's chariot race taking place. In the far side of the hill behind the theatre is the cave where the Seven Brothers and their dog slept for 360 years, and up in the hills to the south is the house in which the Virgin Mary ended her days. In high summer, Ephesus is as busy as Oxford Street — the long bronzed limbs of Scandinavians, urgent guides shepherding their groups in German or Japanese and the click and roll of cameras are a constant distraction from the ruins.

South of Kusadasi are four major historical sites, of which Priene, Miletus and Didyma may be done in an exhausting day, while Heaklia is a bit further away and requires a little longer. All are victims of the silt brought down by the Maeander and its tributaries. 65

Priene, the closest, is perched high on a rock, overlooking what was once sea, but is now alluvial plain; the great columns of its principal temple have been re-erected and are visible for 70 miles, as they were to ships, but no other building stands. The regular grid of its groundplan was imposed on a steeply-sloping site between the acropolis hill and the harbour, and all 75 its public buildings neatly slotted in; it was impregnable from the land side and easily defensible from the sea. The fit and adventurous may attempt the acropolis; the climb is steep and 80 by no means safe for the wobbly and weak-kneed; the view is as breathtaking as the ascent.

Not far from Priene, Miletus rises sharply out of the smooth plain below. 85 The great theatre and the baths built by the wife of Marcus Aurelius (the most complete of all surviving baths) are its principal monuments. Away in a distant corner is an elegant-ly 90 beautiful mosque, clad in white marble, built in 1404 when the city was still alive and part of the Selcuk Empire. Again it makes sense to climb to the highest point — here you 95 will find the Byzantine castle alongside the theatre — and using your imagination, you can make out the old water's edge and the logic of the site.

South of Miletus, Didyma was never 100 a city, merely a temple shrine to Apollo, said by some to be by the same architect as the destroyed Temple of Artemis — it is a pity that this is not so, for it has an awe-inspiring 105 grandeur that gives some inkling of the ancient wonder of the world. It stood intact for nearly 2000 years, and was then felled in 1493 by an earthquake. Three of the gigantic columns 110 and all its internal walls survive to give a clue to its design and purpose, but even the broken remains of the fallen columns are of astounding scale. No single monument in the whole of 115 Turkey has quite such presence.

*(From 'Asia for Beginners' by Brian Sewell;* **Sunday Times Magazine,** *14 December 1985)*

# 4 Language study

### a) Vocabulary: adjectival compounds

*partially-completed / steeply-sloping / week-kneed / breath-taking / awe-inspiring*

Such adjectival compounds are formed from a past or present participle preceded by an adjective, adverb or noun. What are the appropriate compound adjectives for the following?

> an employer who has a hard heart
> an idea that provokes thought
> a business which is expanding rapidly
> an attack which is planned well
> a committee which makes a decision
> a room which is arranged neatly
> an election which has been timed well

### b) Language focus: prepositions and phrases of position

The passage describes the location of some places in Turkey. The following are some of the prepositions and phrases used to describe position:

| | |
|---|---|
| | up          north<br>halfway down the south coast of _____<br>along        east<br>west |
| _____ is (situated)<br>lies | at the mouth of the River _____<br>on the River _____<br>on Lake _____<br>at the foot of Mt _____ |
| | in the N/W/NW etc ⎫ of _____<br>middle/centre ⎬ (country)<br><br>(____ kms) to the N/E/W/S of _____<br>(____ miles) (away) from _____<br>not far from _(place)_ |

### c) Activity

Describe the locations of the ten places marked on the map and their relative position to the capital, Kingston. The first one has been done for you.
A is half way down the west coast, about 100 km from Kingston.

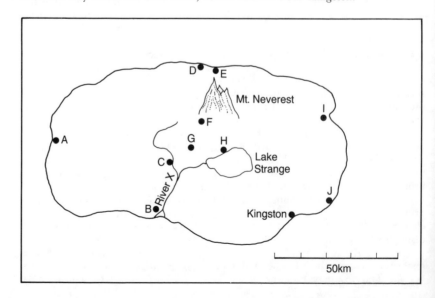

# 5 Transfer

**a) Text**

1 By referring to the text, name the features labelled as letters on the map of Turkey.

2 Mark the route recommended by the writer.

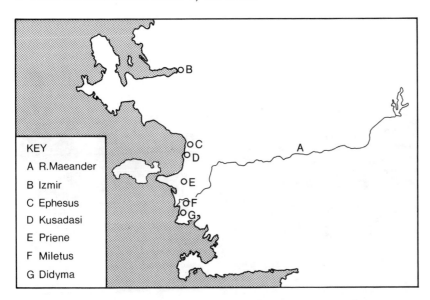

KEY

A R.Maeander

B Izmir

C Ephesus

D Kusadasi

E Priene

F Miletus

G Didyma

**b) Discussion**

People go on holiday for a variety of reasons. Discuss the type of holiday you prefer and what your country has to offer the tourist.

# 6 Writing

**Write about one of these:**

a) Describe the most enjoyable holiday you have had.

b) Plan a two-week trip around your country for a foreign tourist.

# MODULE 5
## GEOGRAPHY C

## 1 Setting the scene

## 2 Vocabulary

| | |
|---|---|
| Harrods /ˈhærədz/ | famous department store in London |
| West End /west ˈend/ | theatre area of London |
| irritate /ˈɪrɪteɪt/ | make angry, annoy |
| bump /bʌmp/ | small raised area |
| unspoilt /ʌnˈspɔɪlt/ | not damaged by man |
| M4 /emˈfɔː/ | motorway running west from London |
| head /hed/ | go in a direction |
| cliffs /klɪfs/ | steep face of rock, especially on a coast |
| coves /kəʊvz/ | small bays |
| Severn /ˈsevən/ | name of a river, dividing England and Wales |
| wilderness /ˈwɪldənes/ | wild, uncultivated land |

## 3 Tape

While listening to the tape, pick out the answers to the following questions:
a)  What is the speaker's main complaint about foreign visitors to Britain?
b)  Which two areas can be reached by using the M4?
c)  Where are the Highlands?

## 4 Language study

**a)  Vocabulary and pronunciation**

Underline the stressed syllable in the following words from the tape:

| | |
|---|---|
| probably | fantastic |
| majority | picturesque |
| ordinary | magnificent |
| especially | awe-inspiring |
| frequently | adventurous |

**b) Useful words and phrases: expressions with 'get'**

Like most English people, the speaker uses the word 'get' a number of times in different ways, often to reinforce the verb 'have', which sounds more formal when used on its own in British English. In more formal or written styles, we avoid 'get' by using other words, often ones based on Latin. Replace the 'get' expressions in the passage below with their more formal equivalents from the list given:

*be admonished / receive / be obliged to / become irritated / manage / influence / someone in one's favour / recover from / continue with / become acquainted with / rise*

*I got up* early yesterday morning, even though I *was just getting over* a rotten cold. But I *had just got* a letter from Mr Biggins, my new boss. He *had got annoyed* that I had not been in the office and was warning me that *I'd got to get on with* my work as quickly as possible. I *was just getting to know* the job and I thought I *was getting along* quite well, so I was surprised to *get told off* as soon as this. But I was sure that if I went to see him I *could get round him* quite easily.

**c) Language focus: '-ever' compounds**

The speaker uses several '-ever' compounds (whenever etc). These are usually pronounced with the stress on the first syllable of '-ever' and have a 'universal' meaning (it doesn't matter who, which etc), occasionally with a slightly perjorative or indifferent sense (Costa del Whatever), or, as question words, expressing surprise or incredulity.

**d) Activity**

Fill in the gaps with the appropriate '-ever' compound:

1  He's so well-known now he's recognised _____ he goes.
2  He says he's suffering from psittacosis, _____ that is.
3  _____ carefully I do it, I still make mistakes.
4  _____ of those boys is responsible, he will be punished.
5  _____ will he think of next?
6  Do drop in and see us _____ you are in town.
7  It's a quotation from P. Higginbottom, _____ he is.
8  _____ did you do such a silly thing?
9  The committee will do _____ is necessary to ensure their success.
10  _____ car is blocking the entrance, could he or she please move it? (careful!)
11  _____ did you buy that hat?
12  _____ I phone them, the line's engaged.

# 5  Transfer

**a) Tape**

Listen to **Section I** again and fill in the blanks in the following sentences:

1  For some foreigners, Wales is just a _____ on the map.
2  In London, all the _____ and _____ seem to be foreigners.
3  _____, it's very easy to get to the National Parks.

From **Section II**, choose the best answer to the following:
1  To get to Devon and Cornwall from the M4, you turn
a)  south.                          b)  west.
c)  east.                           d)  north.

2  The best feature of the beaches is
a)  the warmth.                     b)  the fish.
c)  the lack of crowds.             d)  the sun worshippers.

3  People are sometimes killed on the Yorkshire Moors because
a)  they are not properly equipped.   b)  the mountains are tiny.
c)  they change their minds.          d)  they wonder where to go.

In **Section III**, use the information to make questions to which the following are answers:

a) Four hours.     b)   One person per square mile.
c) A network of slow-moving rivers and lakes.

**b)  Discussion**

Does a capital city give a true picture of a country? Where should tourists go in your country to get a fair impression of it?

# 6   Writing

**Write about one of these:**

a)   The average tourist leaves a country with a completely misleading impression of the place and the people.

b)   Describe any areas of your country you would not recommend a tourist to visit.

# 1 Setting the scene

# 2 Vocabulary

| | |
|---|---|
| drastic /ˈdræstɪk/ | with a strong effect |
| iron ore /ˈaɪən ɔː/ | mineral from which iron is made |
| bitterly /ˈbɪtəlɪ/ | extremely |
| studs /stʌdz/ | metal points |
| grip /grɪp/ | keep a firm hold |
| cope with /ˈkəup wɪð/ | manage successfully |
| reindeer /ˈreɪndɪə/ | large deer (see picture above) |
| lichen /ˈlaɪkən/ or /ˈlɪtʃən/ | small green or grey plant growing on rocks or tree trunks |
| moss /mos/ | similar to lichen, usually found in wet places |
| nomads /ˈnəumædz/ | people who wander from place to place |
| fall-out /ˈfɔːl aut/ | radioactive pollution |

# 3 Tape

On the tape you will hear two people discussing Sweden. While listening to them, find the answers to the following questions:
a) What is the standard image a foreigner has of Sweden?
b) How cold does it get in the Arctic?
c) How did the Chernobyl disaster affect the Lapps?

# 4 Language study

**a) Vocabulary: collective nouns**
The speaker mentions *a flock of geese* and *a herd of reindeer*. We have a great number of such collective words in English. Link the collective word on the left with the appropriate noun on the right:

| | | | |
|---|---|---|---|
| | school | | bananas |
| | gang | | bees |
| | flock | | rioters |
| | pride | | stars |
| a | shoal | of | elephants |
| | swarm | | whales |
| | bunch | | fish |
| | pack | | sheep |
| | mob | | cards |
| | herd | | thieves |
| | galaxy | | lions |

**b) Useful words and phrases: expressions with 'tell'**

One speaker says 'you can tell when you're in the Arctic Circle'.

'Tell' is normally followed by the indirect object (tell someone something), but there are a few phrases where tell is not followed by the indirect object:

*tell the difference / tell ... apart / tell lies / tell the truth / tell tales / tell ... off / tell on ...*

Put each of the above in the correct form into the following sentences:

1  My mother _____ last night for coming home late.
2  The twins are so alike I just _____.
3  Only an expert can _____ between these wines.
4  He's an inveterate liar. He never _____.
5  He has worked too much and the pressure is beginning _____.
6  I simply don't believe you. You are always _____.
7  I don't want to hear what your brother did wrong. You shouldn't _____.

**c) Language focus: order of adjectives**

David had the impression of 'tall, blond, silent Swedes'. We don't often string a number of adjectives together when we speak, but there are rules to help decide the order if we do. The general rule is to place the most specific nearest the head word. The following is a generally accepted order:

| | general | age | colour | participle | origin | noun | head |
|---|---|---|---|---|---|---|---|
| the | fat | old | grey | weeping | Chinese | water | carrier |

Adjectives showing the speaker or writer's attitude normally come before other descriptive adjectives, eg:

an exciting, new, bright yellow children's toy

**d) Activity**

Put the following adjectives in the correct order with the headword given:

1   a ... dog                      big lovely black
2   a ... morning                  frosty cold beautiful
3   this ... sock                  old football smelly
4   the ... system                 early-warning latest American
5   my ... friend                  fishing young keen
6   several ... containers         metal old dangerous
7   our ... suitcases              weekend new lightweight nice
8   a fleet of ... boats           blue battered sailing
9   a ... artist                   street well-known French
10  a squad of ... soldiers        volunteer young smartly-dressed

# 5  Transfer

**a) Tape**

Listen to **Section I** of the tape again.

1 Which of the two speakers has visited Sweden?
   a) Eric       b) John       c) Both       d) Neither

2 How much of Sweden is in the Arctic Circle?
   a) Half       b) One third       c) One fifth       d) One tenth

3 What indicates when you have reached the Arctic Circle?
   a) A drastic change       b) A sudden change
   c) A wooden notice       d) A road sign

In **Section II**, say whether the following are true or false:
1 It is colder underground in the mine.
2 They export all their iron-ore through Luleå.
3 The roads are kept clear of snow in winter.

Choose the best answer for these questions on **Section III**:
1 The Lapps are
   a) tall and blonde.       b) short and blonde.
   c) tall and dark.       d) short and dark.

2 The Lapps
   a) are richer than other Swedes.
   b) live in great comfort.
   c) don't stay in one place.
   d) work in the nuclear industry.

3 The Chernobyl disaster has
   a) brought more work to the Lapps.
   b) made no difference to them.
   c) burnt all their reindeer.
   d) endangered their way of life.

**b) Discussion**
One of the speakers has preconceived ideas about Sweden and its people. Do you feel that your opinions of other countries and nationalities are well-founded? Do some other people have a wrong idea about your country and people?

# 6 Writing

**Write about one of these:**
a) Describe the appearance and character of a typical fellow-countryman.
b) Make a list of recommendations for a foreigner on how to behave correctly in your country.

# MODULE 6
## CULTURAL SURVEY A

## 1 Setting the scene

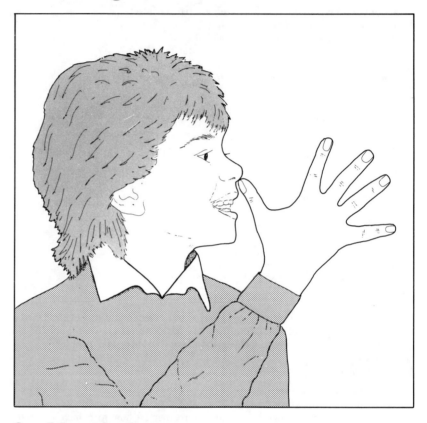

## 2 Vocabulary

| | | |
|---|---|---|
| gesture *n* | (l.3) | movement, usually of the hands, which has a communicative purpose |
| posture *n* | (l.4) | way of holding one's body |
| layman *n* | (l.5) | person who is not a specialist |
| clue *n* | (l.6) | something that helps to find an answer by providing information |
| depict *vt* | (l.8) | show or represent |
| deception *n* | (l.8) | lie |
| deceit *n* | (l.19) | dishonesty |
| vigorously *adv* | (l.20) | forcefully |
| suppress *vt* | (l.31) | prevent from appearing, stop |
| fist *n* | (l.33) | hand with the fingers closed tightly |
| fake *adj/n* | (l.34) | not real, intended to deceive |

## 3 Text

While reading the text find the answers to the following questions:

a) Two parts of the body are particularly associated with deception. What are they?

b) If a listener covers his ears, it indicates that he wishes to 'hear no ...'.

c) What part of the body is traditionally associated with honesty?

# ■ HOW TO TELL IF SOMEONE IS LYING

Communication through body language has been going on for thousands of years, but has only been studied scientifically during the last 30 years or so. Yet more human communication takes place by the use of gestures, postures, positions and distances than most of us realise, say the researchers. All
5 this has practical application for laymen. For instance, body language can provide clues to help you tell when someone is lying. Remember the three wise monkeys who hear, speak and see no evil? The hand-to-face actions they depicted often indicate human deception.

If a young child tells a lie, he frequently covers his mouth with his hands in an
10 attempt to stop the deceitful words from coming out. If he does not wish to listen to a reprimanding parent, he may simply cover his ears with his hands. Similarly, when he sees something he doesn't want to look at, he covers his eyes with his hands or arms. As a person becomes older, the hand-to-face gestures become more refined and less obvious, but they still occur. The
15 following are common gestures that put me on my guard — although they shouldn't be regarded as infallible evidence that someone is lying.

### 1 The Eye Rub

'See no evil' says the wise monkey. This gesture is an attempt to block out the deceit, doubt or lie that a person sees — or to avoid having to look at the face of
20 someone to whom he is telling a lie. Men usually rub their eyes vigorously, and if the lie is a big one they will often look away, normally towards the floor. Women, on the other hand, often use a small, gentle rubbing motion just below the eye, probably to avoid smudging their eye make-up.

### 2 The Neck Scratch

25 The index finger of the writing hand scratches below the ear lobe. My observation of this gesture reveals an interesting point: rarely is the number of scratches more or less than five. This gesture is probably a signal of doubt or uncertainty, characteristic of the person who thinks, 'I'm not sure I agree'.

### 3 The Mouth Guard

30 The hand covers the mouth, and the thumb is pressed against the cheek. It is possible that the brain is subconsciously instructing the hand to suppress the deceitful words that are being said. Sometimes this gesture may be only a few fingers over the mouth, or a closed fist. Some people try to disguise this gesture by giving a fake cough.
35 If a person uses this gesture while speaking to you, it may indicate he is telling a lie. However, if he covers his mouth while you are speaking, it may indicate that he feels *you* are lying!

### 4 The Nose Touch

In essence, this gesture is a sophisticated, disguised version of the mouth guard.
40 It may consist of several light rubs below the nose, or it may be one quick, almost imperceptible touch. One explanation of the origin of this gesture is that, as the negative thought enters the mind, the subconscious instructs the hand to cover the mouth. However, at the last moment, in an attempt to appear less obvious, the hand pulls away from the face. Like the mouth guard, it can be
45 used both by the speaker to disguise his own deceit and by the listener who doubts the speaker's words.

### 5 The Ear Rub

This is an attempt by the listener to 'hear no evil'. Other variations of this gesture include rubbing the back of the ear, pulling at the ear lobe or bending
50 the entire ear forward to cover the ear hole. This last gesture is a signal that the person has heard enough.

### 6 The Open Palm

Throughout history, the open palm, as opposed to the hand-to-face gestures, has been associated with truth, honesty, allegiance and submission. One valuable
55 way to discover whether or not someone is being open and honest is to look for palm displays. When a child is lying or concealing something, his palms are often hidden behind his back.
You may ask, 'Do you mean that if I tell lies with my palms visible, people will believe me?' The answer to this is yes — and no. If you tell an outright lie with

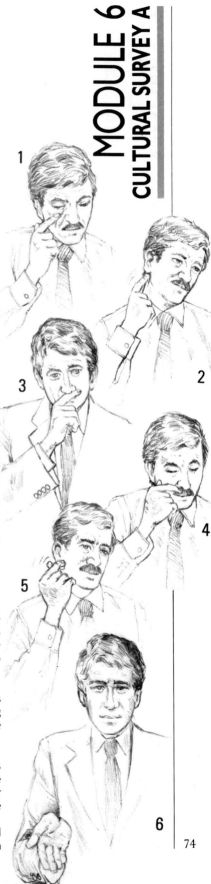

1
2
3
4
5
6

60  your palms exposed, you may still appear insincere because of many other gestures that are inconsistent with the open palms. Despite this, it is possible to make yourself appear more credible by practising open-palm gestures when communicating with others; conversely, as the open-palm gestures become habitual, the tendency to tell untruths lessens. The use of palm signals also en-
65  courages others to be open with you.
Honest!

*(From Body Language: How to Read Others' Thoughts by their Gestures by Alan Pease)*

# 4  Language study

**a)  Vocabulary: honesty and certainty**
The words below are related to the concepts of honesty and certainty.

First complete the table:

| Noun | Adjective |
| --- | --- |
| untruth | |
| doubt | |
| uncertainty | |
| honesty | |
| | insincere |
| | credible |
| | open |
| deception | |
| deceit | |
| | fake |

Now put a + by those adjectives which represent positive attributes; put a — by those adjectives which represent negative attributes; leave neutral adjectives blank.

**b)  Useful words and phrases: phrasal and prepositional verbs**
Look at the phrasal verbs below. Then complete the sentences.

go on            look at            react to
take place       look away          look for

Although the affair had <u>(1)</u>_____ a long time before, she found she still couldn't <u>(2)</u>_____ the photograph without a feeling of sadness. She still <u>(3)</u>_____ it in the same way. Why couldn't she <u>(4)</u>_____ someone else? Finally she <u>(5)</u>_____, tears welling up in her eyes. How could she <u>(6)</u>_____ living?

**c)  Language focus: contrast and opposition**
The text contains a number of markers of **contrast**. These can be classified as follows:

**1  Adverbial links**

An adverbial link connects two ideas normally at the sentence level. Adverbial links of contrast include: however, yet, nevertheless.

Here are some examples from the text:

. . . the subconscious instructs the hand to cover the mouth. However, at the last minute, in an attempt . . .

. . . during the last 30 years or so. Yet more human communication . . .

## 2   Co-ordination between clauses

A co-ordinating conjunction connects two main clauses. 'But' is a co-ordinating conjunction of contrast. Here is an example from the text:

Communication through body language has been going on for thousands of years, but has only been studied scientifically . . .

## 3   Subordination between clauses

A subordinating conjunction introduces a subordinate clause. 'Although' is a subordinating conjunction of contrast. Here is an example from the text:

The following are common gestures that put me on my guard — although they shouldn't be regarded as infallible evidence that someone is lying.

## 4   Prepositional phrases

Prepositional phrases are followed by a noun or pronoun. 'Despite' and 'in spite of' are prepositional phrases of contrast. Here is an example from the text:

Despite this, it is possible to make yourself appear more credible . . .

The text also contains a number of markers of **opposition**:

Women, *on the other hand*, often use a small, gentle rubbing motion . . .
. . . the open palm, *as opposed to* the hand-to-face gestures . . .
. . . by practising open-palm gestures when communicating with others; *conversely*, as the open-palm gestures become habitual . . .

### d)   Activity

Complete the following text, using each of the following markers once:

*yet / although / despite / although / but / on the other hand / as opposed to / however*

(1) _____ some features of body language may be universal, the majority are culture specific. On the one hand there are variations in the features used by different cultures to indicate the same meaning; (2) _____, the same feature may have different meanings in different cultures. Take, for example, insults. In Britain very slow hand-clapping is an insult; (3) _____ in Russia, the same gesture can be highly complimentary. In greetings, (4) _____, the action of embracing is generally interpreted in the same way, (5) _____ with different degrees of physical contact.

# 5   Transfer

**a)**   Link the gestures on the left with the characteristic action on the right:

| Gesture | | Action |
|---|---|---|
| 1   the eye rub | a) | to cover the mouth |
| 2   the neck scratch | b) | to rub lightly above the mouth |
| 3   the mouth guard | c) | to look away |
| 4   the nose touch | d) | to reveal an open palm |
| 5   the ear rub | e) | to scratch below the ear lobe |
| 6   the open palm | f) | to pull at the ear lobe |

### b)   Discussion

What examples of body language are common in your culture? Consider these: greetings and farewells; insults; agreement and disagreement; approval and disapproval; friendship signals

# 6   Writing

**Write about one of these:**
a)   Write a letter to a foreign friend describing some of the hand movements used in communication in your society, and explain their meaning.
b)   Since body language can convey contradictory messages, everybody should talk with their hands behind their backs.

# MODULE 6
## CULTURAL SURVEY B

## 1 Setting the scene

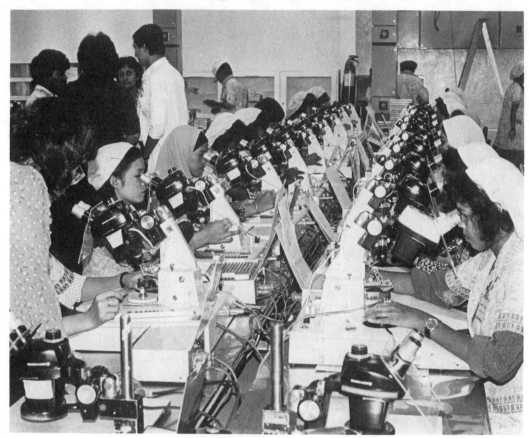

## 2 Vocabulary

| | |
|---|---|
| supplementary *n* (l.13) | additional |
| lay-off *n* (l.15) | redundancy |
| docile *adj* (l.18) | easily controlled |
| manual dexterity *n phr* (l.20) | skill in the use of the hands |
| sabotage *vt* (l.23) | intentionally damage machines |
| nimble *adj* (l.33) | able, agile |
| burgeon *vi* (l.52) | grow |
| subsistence *n* (l.59) | the state of living with little food or money |
| shatter *vt* (l.65) | ruin |

## 3 Text

While reading the text, find the answers to the following questions:

a) What consumer goods does the writer mention that are assembled by women?

b) What type of workforce do multinationals want?

c) What three non-financial benefits do the corporations claim that women get from their working experience?

# ■ WOMEN AND MULTINATIONALS

In the 1800s, farm girls in England and the northeastern United States filled the textile mills of the first Industrial Revolution. Today young Third World women have become the new 'factory girls', providing a vast pool of cheap labour for globe-trotting corporations. Behind the labels 'Made in Taiwan' and 'Assembled in Haiti' may be one of the most strategic blocs of women-power in the 1980s. In the last 15 years many multinational corporations have come to rely on women around the world to keep labour costs down and profits up. Women are the unseen assemblers of consumer goods: toys, the hardware of today's microprocessor revolution, designer jeans. Low wages are the main reason companies move to the Third World. A female assembly line worker in the US is likely to earn between $3.35 and $5 an hour. In many Third World countries a woman doing the same work will earn $3 to $5 a day.

Wage-earning opportunities for women are considered only supplementary income for their families. Management uses that secondary status to pay women less than men, and justify lay-offs during slow periods, claiming that women don't need to work and will probably quit to get married and have babies anyway. Women are the preferred workforce for other reasons too. Multinationals want a workforce that is docile, easily manipulated, and willing to do boring, repetitive assembly work. Women, they claim, are the perfect employees, with their 'natural patience' and 'manual dexterity'. As the personnel manager of an assembly plant in Taiwan says, 'Young male workers are too restless and impatient to be doing monotonous work with no career value. If displeased, they sabotage the machines and even threaten the foremen. But girls, at most they cry a little'. Multinationals prefer single women with no children and no plans to have any. Pregnancy tests are routinely given to potential employees to avoid the issue of maternity benefits.

The majority of the new female workforce is young, between 16 and 25 years old. As one management consultant explains, 'When seniority rises, wages rise,' so the companies prefer to train a fresh group of teenagers rather than give higher pay to experienced women. The youngest workers, usually under 23 years old, are found in electronics and textile factories where keen eyesight and dexterity are essential. A second, older group of women work in industries like food processing where nimble fingers and perfect vision are not required. Multinationals can get away with worse conditions in these factories because the women generally can't get jobs elsewhere.

In their defence, corporations are quick to insist that Third World women are absolutely thrilled with their new-found employment opportunities. A top-level management consultant who advises US companies on where to relocate their factories said, 'The girls genuinely enjoy themselves. They're away from their families. They have spending money. They can buy motor bikes, whatever. Of course it is a regulated experience, too — with dormitories to live in — so it's a healthful experience.' By earning money and working outside the home, factory women may find a certain independence from their families. Meeting and working with other women lays the foundation for a collective spirit and, perhaps, collective action. But at the same time, the factory system relies upon and reinforces the power of men in the traditional patriarchal family to control women.

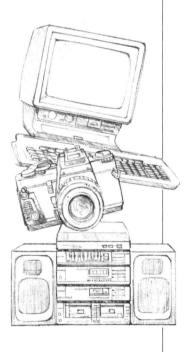

Half a million East Asian women are estimated to be working in export processing zones. Women are heavily employed in export manufacture outside the zones as well. In South Korea, for example, women comprise one-third of the industrial labour force. A great percentage of these 'oriental girls' come from rural areas, drawn to the burgeoning urban centres by reports from friends or older sisters who have landed an assembly job. Companies often recruit in the countryside as well, frequently enlisting the help of village authorities and the fathers and brothers of factory-age women. In Taiwan, large companies work with junior high school principals who offer up bus-loads of recent graduates to labour-hungry plants. For the majority of women, it is their first job experience. They may even be the first wage-earners in their families. The majority of the women earn subsistence-level incomes, whether they work for a multinational corporation or a locally owned factory. While corporate executives insist that the wages are ample in view of the lower standards of living, the minimum wage in most East Asian countries comes nowhere near to covering basic living costs.

65 Subsistence wages are only part of the picture. Most women work under conditions that can break their health or shatter their nerves within a few years, often before they have worked long enough to earn more than a subsistence wage.

*from 'Women and Multinationals' from* **World View**
*edited by P Ayrton and T Engel-hardt*

# 4 Language study

### a) Vocabulary: the financial equation
Tick those words or expressions from the list below which are in the interests of the multinational corporations:

> cheap labour
> to keep labour costs down
> to keep profits up
> low wages
> supplementary income
> to give higher pay
> wage-earner
> subsistence-level income
> maternity benefits
> lower standards of living

### b) Useful words and phrases: companies and factories
The following words from the text describe companies and factories. Link the word on the left with its definition on the right:

| | | | |
|---|---|---|---|
| 1 | mill | a) | a building where goods are made |
| 2 | corporation | b) | factories and large organisations generally |
| 3 | company | c) | a factory, especially in the textile industry |
| 4 | multinational | d) | (machinery in) a factory |
| 5 | factory | e) | a group of people combined together for business |
| 6 | industry | f) | a body comprising many individuals, a big organisation |
| 7 | plant | g) | a very large company with operations in many countries |

### c) Language focus: noun compounds
The text contains a number of noun compounds. In English the headword in such compounds is always in final position; the noun in initial position is normally in the singular,

eg   woman-power (the power of women)
taxpayer (the payer of taxes)
toy factory (a factory which produces toys)

As you can see above, some of the compounds are written as one word, some as two words and some are hyphenated. As the language is continually changing in this area, there are no fixed rules.

### d) Activity
What are noun compounds for the following? The first one has been done for you:

| | |
|---|---|
| Girls who work on farms | farm girls |
| Mills which produce textiles | _____ |
| The costs of labour | _____ |
| Goods intended for consumers | _____ |
| The power provided by men | _____ |

Work done by hand _____

Loads of passengers on buses _____

People who earn wages _____

A building which scrapes the sky _____

A spoon used with tea _____

# 5  Transfer

**a)  Text**
Complete the following table:

| | |
|---|---|
| Hourly pay of assembly line worker in the US | _____ |
| Daily pay of assembly line worker in many Third World countries | _____ |
| Preferred status of female worker in Third World countries | _____ |
| Preferred age range of female workers in Third World countries | _____ |
| Industries for youngest female workers | _____ |
| Fraction of factory workers in South Korea who are women | _____ |

**b)  Discussion**
Women are the natural choice for assembly line jobs.
Who perform these jobs in your country? What are the pay and conditions like?

# 6  Writing

**Write about one of these:**
a)  Write a letter to a foreign friend describing the jobs done by the women in your society.
b)  All societies are basically matriarchal.

# MODULE 6
## CULTURAL SURVEY C

## 1 Setting the scene

## 2 Vocabulary

| | |
|---|---|
| come to terms with /kʌm tə təːmz wɪð/ | accept |
| multilingual /mʌltɪˈlɪŋgwəl/ | containing many languages |
| host /həust/ | country (or person) which receives residents from abroad |
| pluralism /ˈpluərəlɪzəm/ | principle that people of different races and religions can live together peacefully in the same society |
| cohesion /kəuˈhiːʒən/ | ability to stick or live together |
| resources /rɪˈzɔːsɪz/ | facilities |
| resource /rɪˈzɔːs/ | asset or benefit |
| stability /stəˈbɪlətɪ/ | state of being firmly fixed and steady |
| identity /aɪˈdentətɪ/ | individuality |
| erode /əˈrəud/ | become worn away, be lost |
| integration /ɪntəˈgreɪʃən/ | policy not to separate or segregate |
| manifestation /mænɪfesˈteɪʃən/ | that which shows something |
| enhance /enˈhɑːns/ | improve |

## 3 Tape

On the tape you will hear a discussion about multiculturalism in Britain. The speaker assesses the importance of recognising the need to accommodate different cultural groups in Britain, and then goes on to describe how Britain can best achieve the desired goals.

As you listen, answer the following questions.

a) What, according to the speaker, is essential for Britain to be able to function in the future?

b) The speaker says that two skills or areas of knowledge are important for non-native groups. One is the language. What is the other?

c) What percentage of children in London speak a language other than English at home?

# 4 Language study

## a) Vocabulary and pronunciation

Underline the stressed syllable in the following words from the tape. Then complete the word table:

| Adjective | Noun |
|-----------|------|
| important | |
| beneficial | |
| essential | |
| successful | |
| available | |
| extensive | |
| valuable | |
| sensible | |

## b) Useful words and phrases: completeness and incompleteness

The following words and expressions indicate points on a scale between completeness and incompleteness:

to a certain extent
the full scale
little or nothing
fully
to all intents and purposes
extensive

Complete the following sentences using one word or expression from the list above in each gap:

1  I _____ agree with you.
2  I agree with you _____, but not entirely.
3  _____ this matter is now closed.
4  Despite _____ investigations, we have achieved _____.
5  I don't think you really appreciate _____ of the issue.

## c) Language focus: adjective patterns

Adjectives can take three types of complement, as follows:

**1  prepositional phrase:**
   — aware of the scale
   — beneficial to us
   — essential to a people's cultural identity
   — successful in meeting that need
   — valuable to us
   — sensible for us

**2  'that' clause**
   a)  with a personal subject:
   — the various cultures are sure (that) they can communicate
   — I'm sure (that) this has been recognised
   — I am now concerned that practical steps should be taken

   b)  with an introductory 'it' as subject:
   — it is important that we come to terms
   — it is essential that there are both academic and practical facilities

**3  with a 'to' + infinitive:**
   a)  with a personal subject
   — we're likely to be able to

b) with an introductory 'it' as subject:
— it's very easy for it to erode
— it's very difficult to learn another language
— it would seem sensible for us to protect

Notice the use of 'for' in the above sentence. 'We' is the notional subject of 'protect', but because of the infinitive form we must raise the 'we' to the main clause, where it takes the form 'us' after the preposition 'for'.

**d) Activity**

Select the correct answer:

1  I am convinced _____ better resources in education.
   a) of the need for    b) to need

2  In fact I am disappointed _____ have them already.
   a) to not    b) that we don't

3  _____ alarming that so much money is spent in other areas.
   a) It is    b) I am

4  The authorities _____.
   a) are difficult to persuade    b) are difficult in persuading

5  But we are likely _____ in the end.
   a) that we will succeed    b) to succeed

6  So at the moment _____ regrettable that I can't give you a firm answer.
   a) it is    b) I am

7  But I am hopeful _____ succeeding in the future.
   a) for    b) of

8  And I am anxious _____ sort this matter out.
   a) to    b) that I

9  _____ essential for us to take action as soon as possible.
   a) We are    b) It is

10 So it is more than likely _____ reach a successful conclusion.
   a) that we will    b) for us to

# 5  Transfer

**a) Tape**

Listen to the tape again and complete the following table:

| A Multicultural Society | |
|---|---|
| Results of linguistic pluralism for the whole society | _____ |
| Reasons for importance of bilingualism within each linguistic group | _____ |
| Original policy in the UK towards non-English-speaking communities | _____ |
| Necessary condition for learning a foreign language | _____ |
| Main languages taught in British schools | _____ |
| Main uses of these languages | _____ |
| Trading areas for the UK in the future | _____ |

**b) Discussion**

Discuss the position of different cultural and linguistic groups in your country. What do you think the educational and social policies should be for such groups?

# 6  Writing

**Write about one of these:**

a) Describe the different cultural and linguistic groups in your country.

b) The more cultural and linguistic groups in a country, the richer the society.

## 1  Setting the scene

## 2  Vocabulary

| | |
|---|---|
| sedentary /ˈsedəntərɪ/ | settled |
| nomadic /nəʊˈmædɪk/ | wandering |
| exodus /ˈeksədəs/ | departure of a large number of people |
| legendary /ˈledʒəndərɪ/ | having small basis of truth |
| terrain /təˈreɪn/ | land |
| degenerate /dɪˈdʒenəreɪt/ | become worse |
| fringe /frɪndʒ/ | edge |
| feudal /ˈfjuːdəl/ | based on the relationship between master and servant |
| irreplaceable /ɪrəˈpleɪsebəl/ | very special, cannot be replaced |
| livelihood /ˈlaɪvlɪhud/ | means of earning a living |

## 3  Tape

This listening text deals with the gypsies of Europe — their origins and status today.

While you are listening to the tape, find the answers to the following questions:
a)  Where are the gypsies believed to have originated?
b)  From which country's name is the word 'gypsy' derived?
c)  According to the speaker how long have the gypsies been in Europe?

## 4  Language study

**a)  Vocabulary and pronunciation: movement and location**
The following list of words taken from the tape deal with the areas of movement and location. First, underline the syllable which carries the word stress. Then

classify the words into those which indicate movement (M) and those which indicate location (L).

migration (　)
terrain (　)
environment (　)
journey (　)
exodus (　)
centre (　)
arrival (　)
voyage (　)
area (　)
region (　)

**b) Useful words and phrases: points of a compass**

The speaker also uses a number of words indicating direction or location in relation to the points on the compass,

eg   northeastern, westwards, northeast, western, eastern, westward, east

Which of the above words fit into the following sentences? (Note that one word may fit into more than one sentence.)

1   They took the _____ route. (adjective of direction)
2   They arrived in _____ countries. (adjective of location)
3   They travelled _____. (adverb of direction)
4   They stayed in the _____ of the country. (noun of location)
5   They travelled to the _____ of the country. (noun of direction)

**c) Language focus: degrees of certainty**

The following words/expressions were used by the speaker to make deductions or assumptions about the gypsies' past and future. These words/expressions indicate the degree of certainty, probability or uncertainty that the speaker wished to convey.

| | |
|---|---|
| **Certainty** | it is certain that . . .<br>a positive link<br>it conclusively establishes . . .<br>from reliable sources<br>we are sure that . . .<br>beyond doubt<br>the language was definitely influenced . . .<br>of course<br>there is no doubt that . . .<br>their way of life is bound to . . . |
| **Probability** | it seems likely that . . .<br>probably<br>many people assume . . .<br>in all probability<br>as likely as not |
| **Uncertainty** | there is some doubt<br>it is shrouded in mystery |

**d) Activity**

Complete the following text using the words/notes given in brackets at the end of each clause/sentence:

Exactly how the Pyramids were constructed _(1)_____ (shroud/mystery). _(2)_____ that enormous resources of manpower were available (no doubt), and _(3)_____ that the designers could count upon the support of a large workforce (likely). But numbers alone can't _(4)_____ account for the precision of the Pyramids' assembly (conclusive). _(5)_____ that today's technology could recreate such accuracy (certain), but _(6)_____ the technological equipment did not exist in those days (sure), even if the know-how did. So the mystery of their construction will, (7)_____, remain an open question (likely/not).

Some adjectives which indicate degree of certainty can be used personally and impersonally, eg certain; others can be used personally only, eg convinced; and yet others impersonally only, eg definite.

Compare the following sentences:
I am/It is *certain* that gypsies originated ... (Personal and impersonal)
I am *convinced* that gypsies originated ... (Personal)
It is *definite* that gypsies originated ... (Impersonal)
Now indicate the category of the following adjectives using (P) or (I):

    sure
    positive
    confident
    probable
    likely
    possible

# 5 Transfer

**a) Tape**
Complete the following table:

| Profile of Gypsies | |
|---|---|
| Country of origin | |
| Approximate start of westward migration | |
| Country of first recorded stay | |
| European country of longest stay | |
| Main centres of population in Europe today | |
| Traditional occupations | |
| Historical cause of conflicts with urban craftsmen | |
| Economic result of these conflicts | |

**b) Discussion**
Is assimilation the only way by which minority groups can survive?

# 6 Writing

**Write about one of these:**
a) Describe the background and way of life of a minority group in your country.
b) Do you think that minority groups must assimilate in order to survive? Give your reasons for or against.

# MODULE 7
## TRADITIONS A

## 1 Setting the scene

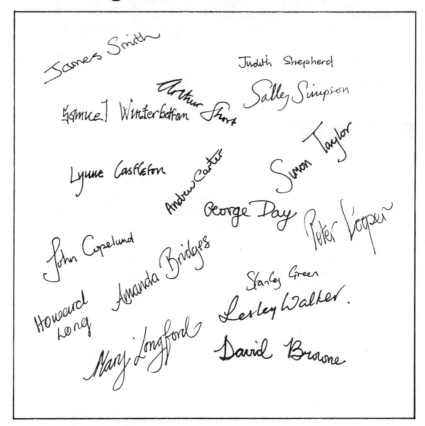

## 2 Vocabulary

| | | |
|---|---|---|
| epithet *n* | (l.2) | descriptive name |
| patronymic *adj* | (l.3) | (name) derived from the name of a father |
| heritable *adj* | (l.4) | (of name, property) which can be passed on to one's descendants |
| stability *n* | (l.9) | state of steadiness, firmness |
| font *n* | (l.10) | place in church where babies are christened |
| thrust *vt* | (l.12) | push violently |
| crudely *adv* | (l.35) | roughly, unskilfully |
| supplant *vt* | (l.43) | replace |
| testify *vi* | (l.52) | provide proof |
| gravity *n* | (l.56) | seriousness |
| circumspection *n* | (l.59) | careful consideration |
| antonym *n* | (l.62) | opposite |
| enclosure *n* | (l.69) | piece of land which is enclosed |

## 3 Text

While reading the text, find the answers to these questions:
a) In Chaucer's time by which name would a man be known?
b) What are the four main types of British surnames?
c) From which of the above types do most British surnames come?

# ■ ENGLISH NAMES

The men and women of Anglo-Saxon England normally bore one name only. Distinguishing epithets were rarely added. These might be patronymic, descriptive, titular or occupational. They were, however, hardly surnames. Heritable names gradually became general in the three centuries following the Norman Conquest. It was not until the 13th and 14th centuries and the two or three generations before Geoffrey Chaucer (Modern French 'Chausseur' — shoe-maker) that surnames became fixed, although for many years after that, the degree of stability in family names varied considerably in different parts of the country. Even in Chaucer's day (c. 1340–1400) the font name was still *the* name and in the course of his life a man might assume many non-font names or, yet more likely, have them thrust upon him by his friends and acquaintances. Servants and apprentices might be known by the name of their masters. 'Richards' may mean 'Richard's man' as well as 'Richard's son'.

Let us imagine a tall young Englishman called 'John' is living in the 13th century by the Green in the village of Hale in the county of the Palatine of Lancaster. He earns his livelihood mainly by making wains or wagons for neighbouring farms. His father's name is 'Peter'. He himself is plain 'John' and frankly, he inclines to resent being called by any other name. But there are several other 'Johns' in the neighbourhood from whom our John must somehow be distinguished in daily conversation although, should he deliver his well-made haywains at outlying farms, he may sometimes be greeted as 'John Peterson of Hale'. He is, to be sure, 'John Peterson Long at Hale Green Wainwright' and as long as he lives, he may be known by any single one or by any combination of these five occasional surnames. Were 'John's' own children to be named after him, they and their descendants might be known as 'Johnson, Jones', 'Jackson', 'Jennings', or even 'Hancock' (all derivatives from 'John'). John's tallness might be commemorated in 'Long', 'Lang' or 'Laing'; or his dwelling by the village centre in 'Green'; or the name of the village in 'Hale'; or his chosen handicraft in 'Wainwright', 'Wright' or 'Smith'.

British surnames fall mainly into four broad categories: patronymic, occupational, descriptive and local. A few names, it is true, will remain puzzling: foreign names, perhaps, crudely translated, adapted or abbreviated: or artificial names.

In fact, over fifty per cent of genuine British surnames derive from place names of different kinds, and so they belong to the last of our four main categories. Even such a name as Simpson may belong to this last group, and not to the first, had the family once had its home in the ancient village of that name in Berkshire, the Swinestone of Domesday Book. Otherwise Simpson means 'the son of Simon or Simeon', as might be expected, the Scandinavian -son gradually supplanting the Old English patronymic -ing. The original Christian name may be unchanged or little changed, as in the typically English names Johnson and Wilson, or it may be modified as in Addison, son of Adam, or Anderson, of Andrew. In Gaelic the prefix is 'Mac-', and so we may associate MacGregor with Gregson, and MacTavish with Davidson.

Hundreds of occupational surnames are at once familiar to us, or at least recognisable after a little thought: Archer, Baxter, Carter, Fisher, Mason, Thatcher, Taylor. Hundreds of others are more obscure in their signification and testify to the amazing specialisation in medieval arts, crafts and functions. Such are 'Amner' (almoner, keeper of the cupboard), 'Bond', (Old Norse for farmer), 'Day', (Old English for breadmaker), and 'Walker', (a fuller of cloth).

All these vocational names carry with them a certain gravity and dignity, which descriptive names often lack. Some, it is true, like 'Long' and 'Lang', 'Short' and 'Little', are simple. They may be taken quite literally. Others require more circumspection: their meanings are slightly different from the modern ones. 'Black' and 'White' implied dark and fair respectively. 'Sharp' meant genuinely discerning, alert, acute rather than quick-

*Mr Charles Short and Mr James Long — but which is which?*

88

witted or clever, and its antonym 'Blunt' signified insensitive, dull, obtuse rather than plain-spoken, abrupt.

65 Place-names have an abiding interest since there is hardly a town or village in all England that has not at some time given its name to a family. They may be picturesque, even poetical: or they may be pedestrian, even trivial. Among the commoner names which survive with relatively little change from old-English times are 'Anstey' (narrow path), 'Milton' (middle enclosure), 'Burton' (fortified enclosure), and 'Hilton'
70 (enclosure on a hill).

*(From Our Language by Simeon Potter)*

# 4 Language study

### a) Vocabulary: verbs of change
The following verbs taken from the text deal with the area of *change*. First connect the verb on the left with its definition on the right:

| | | | |
|---|---|---|---|
| 1 | vary | a) | change by making shorter |
| 2 | adapt | b) | change slightly |
| 3 | abbreviate | c) | be different |
| 4 | translate | d) | change so as to be suitable for different conditions |
| 5 | modify | e) | change into another language |

Now use a part of speech derived from each of the above verbs to complete the following sentences:

English surnames reveal much about the history both of the individual and the country. You may find many (1)_____ in spellings of the same name, some may be (2)_____ of much longer names, others may be slightly (3)_____ from the name of a place, but they all have a history. Even foreign names, which may be retained or (4)_____ (such as Mountbatten from Battenberg), or have a (5)_____ spelling to look more English, can reflect personal or national historical events.

### b) Useful words and phrases: sentence adverbials
Sentence adverbials, as their name implies, modify a sentence rather than one element in it. As such they are peripheral to sentence structure, and frequently stand in front-position,
eg '... and frankly, he inclines to resent being called by any other name.'
Sentence adverbials have a wide range of possible structures, as the following alternatives indicate:

| | | |
|---|---|---|
| 1 | a prepositional phrase | in all frankness |
| 2 | an infinitive phrase | to be frank, to speak frankly |
| 3 | an -ing participle phrase | frankly speaking |
| 4 | a finite verb clause | if I may be frank |

Complete the following list using similar sentence adverbials with 'truthful'. The first one has been done for you.
1 in all truthfulness
2
3
4

### c) Language focus: verb-headed conditionals
The passage contains examples of conditional sentences which start with a verb, eg 'had ...' (l.40), 'were ...' (l.27), and 'should' (l.23). In more formal English, the 'if' of the conditional clause can be replaced by bringing an appropriate verb to the beginning of the sentence:
In Conditional III, we find 'Even such a name as Simpson may belong to this last group, *had* the family had its home in the ancient village ....'
In Conditional II, we find '*Were* 'John's' own children to be named after him, they and their descendants .....'
In Conditional I we find '*Should* he deliver his well-made haywains at outlying farms, he may sometimes be greeted .....'.

**d) Activity**

Rewrite the following sentences as conditionals, starting with a verb. The first one has been done for you.

1 He arrived late so he missed the bus.
  Had he not arrived late, he would not have missed the bus.

2 If he walked in at this moment, we should soon know the answer.

3 You didn't phone me, so I couldn't make the arrangements.

4 He is not sympathetic, so I can't approach him.

5 I am not in a position to help, so I can't.

6 He will inform us immediately if he changes his mind.

7 You are such a liar that I don't believe you.

8 I don't have the means, so I won't buy it.

9 I didn't tell him because he didn't ask.

10 He doesn't have the courage, so he can't do it.

11 If he phones, please tell him I'm out.

12 He was sacked because the project failed.

# 5 Transfer

**a) Text**

Tick the appropriate column below to indicate the derivation of the following surnames:

| Surname | Patronymic | Occupational | Descriptive | Local |
|---|---|---|---|---|
| Andrews | | | | |
| Weaver | | | | |
| Farmer | | | | |
| Greenfield | | | | |
| Whitehead | | | | |
| Kennedy | | | | |
| Parkinson | | | | |
| Southwood | | | | |

**b) Discussion**

In Britain the hyphenated or double-barrelled name, such as Douglas-Home or Fortescue-Smythe, are often indicators of social class. In what ways are names in your country an indicator of origins or social position?

# 6 Writing

**Write about one of these:**

a) Describe the traditional system for naming people in your country.
b) Discuss the origin of some of the names used in your country.

# MODULE 7
## TRADITIONS B

## 1 Setting the scene

## 2 Vocabulary

cacophonous *adj* (l.10)    noisy
priceless *adj* (l.12)    of very great value
crumbling *adj* (l.12)    breaking into small pieces
thoroughfare *n* (l.19)    street
lane *n* (l.22)    small street
trap *vt* (l.24)    to prevent from escaping
crooked *adj* (l.26)    not straight
remnant *n* (l.28)    what is left when everything else has gone
crenellated *adj* (l.29)    shaped like the top of castle walls:
vendor *n* (l.36)    a person selling something
jostle *v* (l.38)    to knock or push (people)
prosper *vi* (l.70)    to become rich and successful
moucharaby *n* (l.105)    a balcony enclosed by lattice work
embellishment *n* (l.118)    extra decoration

## 3 Text

While reading the text, find the answers to these questions:
a) What does the writer find most attractive about Cairo?
b) What does he see as the biggest problem?
c) What is the solution to this problem?

# ■ City of a Thousand Minarets

On a clear day, from the heights of the massive twelfth century citadel that overlooks Cairo, you can see forever — or at least for most of recorded history.

Far away in the western desert are the ancient pyramids of Giza. Closer in, the glass-walled skyscrapers run parallel to the Nile. Below, almost submerged within the cacophonous streets of modern Cairo, are the priceless crumbling remains of the old metropolis, once one of the medieval world's greatest cities, a fabulous place of inns, bazaars, hospitals, public fountains and baths.

To find the old city, you must go on foot. Pass through twin gates to the main thoroughfare, Qasabat al Qahira, as it was known in medieval times. Beyond are narrow cobbled lanes that protect Cairo's citizens from the sun and hot desert wind by giving shade and trapping the cool night air.

The crooked streets have wonders to reveal. Behind broken facades there is splendour — remnants of crenellated walls, massive stone domes and soaring minarets.

The great palace of the Fatimid conquerors from Tunisia, who laid out the city in AD 969, has long since disappeared, but the crowds flowing along the Qasabat have not. The street is a huge bazaar with vendors selling everything from garlic to gold.

Amid the jostling humanity are figures that seem to leap from the past. The mibkharah, in a flowing striped gown, with a long grey beard and ruby-heaped fingers, performs his ancient task of incensing shops and homes, offering a prayer and receiving a few piastres in return. The sakkah, or water carrier, pushes through the crowd with a dripping goatskin on his back.

History records that 12,000 water carriers with 15,000 camels went to the Nile twice a day to fetch water. Many alleyways were too narrow for the camels, so the sakkah delivered water to the door. Payment was due upon delivery, which meant the sick and poor could die of thirst. And so it became the pious custom for sultans, princes and merchants to donate beautiful sabils, or public drinking fountains, which were adorned with verses from the Koran and bore the donor's name. In medieval Cairo there were perhaps 100 of these ornate public fountains. Today, many are in ruins, but dozens still exist although none is in use.

Where did the princes get the money for the sabils? From the thirteenth to the fifteenth centuries, Cairo prospered as few cities have done — thanks to the Mamelukes, a corps of warriors who ruled Egypt for nearly three centuries, and the city's virtual monopoly on trade between Asia and Europe.

Ships came along the Red Sea bearing spices, silks and porcelain from the East and the goods were then taken overland to Cairo. Western merchants arrived to trade their goods for jewels, silk and spices. By the fourteenth century, most of the spices from the East destined for European kitchens passed through Cairo.

With so many long-distance travellers entering and leaving Cairo, the Street of the Camel Saddlers did a roaring business, as did the Bazaar of the Armourers. These have long since disappeared, but today in small rooms and courtyards throughout the city the inheritors of many other medieval skills ply their trade.

All day long a chorus of banging comes from the coppersmiths' bazaar, a gentler tapping from the brass and silversmiths and a soft roar from the glass-blowers' straw furnaces.

In the Street of the Tentmakers a few skilled craftsmen still painstakingly sew huge appliqued tent pavilions or sewans. Nearby is the Street of the Woodworkers, where the intricately carved moucharaby screens that once adorned thousands of Cairo's windows are made. The Street of the Musical Instruments houses craftsmen who fashion flutes, drums, tambourines and lutes.

Many of Cairo's surviving wonders are architectural, and during the centuries when the sultans were building monuments to themselves, Cairo's master masons designed more and more intricate patterns on stone, wood and ivory. After five centuries of embellishment Cairo stood adorned like no other city on earth.

But today Cairo is a victim of time and neglect. Every month another wall falls, another dome cracks and,

92

as their houses collapse around them, the inhabitants camp in mosques and tombs.

In 1979 UNESCO declared medieval Cairo a treasure to be preserved for all mankind, and work was begun to restore some of the more important buildings. These edifices are all a part of the world's heritage. The 'City of a Thousand Minarets' must not be allowed to crumble.

*(From **Reader's Digest** © 1984; article by John Feeny)*

# 4  Language study

### a)  Vocabulary: buildings and parts or buildings

The passage uses the following words to describe buildings or parts of buildings. Place them in the appropriate box according to whether they are whole or parts of buildings:

| minaret | dome | pyramid | facade |
|---|---|---|---|
| skyscraper | mosque | inn | courtyard |
| bazaar | citadel | hospital | edifice |

| Whole building | Part of building |
|---|---|
|  |  |

### b)  Useful words and phrases: collocations

Each of the following adjectives is often collocated with one of the nouns given from the passage. Put them into appropriate pairs. The first answer is 1 e).

| | | | |
|---|---|---|---|
| 1 | crooked | a) | patterns |
| 2 | ornate | b) | remains |
| 3 | intricate | c) | citadels |
| 4 | long-distance | d) | business |
| 5 | glass-walled | e) | streets |
| 6 | massive | f) | fountains |
| 7 | crumbling | g) | minarets |
| 8 | roaring | h) | travellers |
| 9 | soaring | i) | skyscrapers |

### c)  Language focus: inversion after adverbials of place

In order to change the focus of the sentence, the writer has occasionally started with an adverbial and inverted the subject and verb. The first example is: 'Below, almost submerged within the cacophonous streets of Cairo, *are* the priceless, crumbling remains of the old metropolis . . .'. The verbs in this type of construction are normally intransitive.

### d)  Activity

**1**  Rewrite the following sentences, starting with an adverbial and inverting the subject and verb. The first one has been done for you.

1  A dusty old piano stood in the corner.
   In the corner stood a dusty old piano.

2  A gnarled old oak tree grew outside the back door.
   _____

3  A crowd of festive holiday makers danced down the road.
   _____

4  A note from John was hidden among the flowers.
   _____

5  A loud scream came from behind the locked door.
   _____

6  A diamond ring lay in the centre of the cushion.
   _____

7    A timid little mouse peeped through the hole.

8    A tall man with a handlebar moustache was standing next to the host.

9    A very irate detective strode into the room.

10    A magnificent portrait of his grandfather hung above the fireplace.

**2**    Make up ten sentences to describe the picture below, starting with an abverbial and inverting the subject and verb (imagine it is part of a novel and write your sentences in the past).

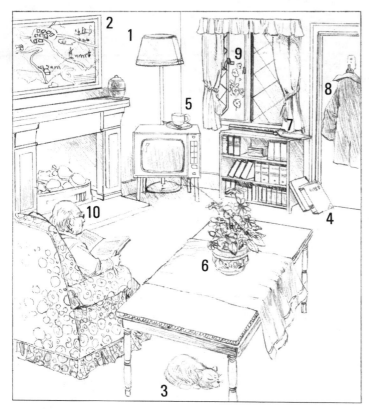

# 5    Transfer

**a)   Text**
The writer gives colour to the text by using several local words not normally found in English. Check back through the passage and give the meanings of the following:

*mibkharah* (1.40)          *sabil* (1.59)          *sewan* (1.103)
*sakkah* (1.45)          *Mameluke* (1.71)

Are any of them in your English dictionary?

**b)   Discussion**
Many old city centres are unsuitable for modern life. Should they be knocked down and replaced or preserved?

# 6    Writing

**Write about one of these:**
a)   Describe one of the most famous monuments or buildings in your country.
b)   City life is far more exciting and interesting than living in the country.

# MODULE 7
## TRADITIONS C

## 1 Setting the scene

## 2 Vocabulary

| | | |
|---|---|---|
| put on | /put on/ | bet money |
| bet | /bet/ | try to win money on a future event |
| fancy | /ˈfænsɪ/ | like |
| outing | /ˈautɪŋ/ | race |
| going | /ˈgəuɪŋ/ | condition of the race track |
| tip | /tɪp/ | advice from an expert |
| toss-up | /ˈtos ʌp/ | an equal chance |
| counter | /ˈkauntə/ | a flat surface for working in a shop |
| slip | /slɪp/ | form, printed piece of paper |
| bookmaker | /ˈbukmeɪkə/ | person who takes bets |
| odds | /odz/ | ratio of money bet to money won, degree of probability |
| outsider | /autˈsaɪdə/ | an unknown competitor with little chance of winning |

## 3 Tape

On the tape, you will hear two men discussing how to bet on horse races. As you listen, answer the following questons:
a) Does Charlie make a profit from his betting?
b) How does he decide which horse to bet on?
c) Why does his friend bet on Suzie Who?

## 4 Language study

**a) Vocabulary and pronunciation: English money**

In spoken English, there are several terms to refer to money. For sums less than £1, we usually say simply 'p', eg 5p, 10p etc. Over £1, we say 'three pounds twenty', or 'eight pounds seventy-five' and so on. We never say 'six-and-a-half pounds', because that suggests weight (6lb 8oz) — it is 'six pounds fifty'. What do the following mean?

*a fiver / a tenner / a quid / coppers / loose change / small change / folding money*

In 1971, Britain changed from an old system to a decimal system, but you may still hear or read about the old coinage. Do you know what the following mean?

*shilling / bob / tanner / half-a-crown / florin*

**b) Useful words and phrases: expressions with 'odd'**

The word 'odds' is used here in a very specific sense. Its use in betting has given rise to a number of expressions in everyday English. But the word 'odd' has several other meanings. Complete the following sentences with one of these phrases:

*at odds / against the odds / odds and ends / feeling odd / an odd number / odds-on favourite / the odd occasion / the odd man out*

1  We can't divide the group into two equal teams because we are _____.
2  Cow, sheep, pig, crocodile: which is _____?
3  It's no use trying to get them to agree. They're always _____ with each other.
4  They were sure that Margaret Thatcher was the _____ to be next Prime Minister.
5  I don't really know Paris all that well. I've only been there on _____.
6  Sue says she's _____. It must be the seafood she had for lunch.
7  I doubt if he'll turn up. Given this weather, it's _____.
8  I didn't find much in the drawer — only _____.

## c)  Language focus: short answers

Transitive verbs normally have an object, even when in short responses. This can be the appropriate pronoun: eg   I don't want one.
Verbs taking an infinitive construction retain the particle 'to': eg   I asked him to.
Verbs of thinking or speaking use 'so': eg   I think so — I told you so.
Note: The informal negative with 'think' is: I don't think so ('I think not' is more formal).

## d)  Activity

Give a short response to the following questions, using the verb given and making your answer positive or negative according to the sign:
eg   Why do you bet on horses? (+ enjoy) — I enjoy it.
     Did you do that? (− do) − No, I didn't do it.
1  Why didn't you come last night? (− feel like)
2  Why aren't you going to the match? (− be allowed)
3  Is he going to win? (+ hope)
4  Why didn't you sign your name? (+ forget)
5  Have you eaten all those chocolates? (+ like)
6  Are you going to do this exercise? (− want)
7  Will it rain tomorrow? (+ expect)
8  Did you break that window? (− intend)
9  Have you got a pen? (− have got)
10  Why did you close the door? (+ be told)

# 5   Transfer

## a)  Tape

Listen to the tape again and then look at the following race card:

| | | | |
|---|---|---|---|
| Beginner's Luck | 100–30 | The Insider | 14–1 |
| Last Chance | 12–4 | Fool's Paradise | 2–1 |
| Headstart | 5–4 on | Long Shot | 7–4 |

1  Which horse has the longest odds?
2  Which is the favourite?
3  For each horse in turn, if you bet £1, how much would you win if it won?

## b)  Discussion

Betting is a very popular sport in England, although it was illegal for years. Is betting allowed in your country? What is the most popular form of betting? What kind of things can you bet on?

# 6   Writing

### Write about one of these:

a)  Explain what you would do if you won £10,000.
b)  Gambling is dangerous and should be made illegal.

# MODULE 7
## TRADITIONS D

## 1  Setting the scene

## 2  Vocabulary

| | |
|---|---|
| converted /kən'və:tɪd/ | persuaded to accept |
| amulet /'æmjulet/ | objects worn to protect against evil |
| pendant /'pendənt/ | ornament hanging from the neck |
| trappings /'træpɪŋz/ | articles worn as a sign of position |
| endowed /en'daud/ | given (of special qualities) |
| ward off /wɔ:d of/ | keep away, prevent |
| curse /'kə:s/ | harm or evil called down by an enemy |
| fee /fi:/ | money paid for services |
| valid /'vælɪd/ | having a firm base |
| ritual /'rɪtjuəl/ | repeated religious ceremony or action |
| gourd /guəd/ | outer shell of large fruit used as a bowl or container |

## 3  Tape

On this tape, an Englishman is talking about his experiences in Togo, West Africa. While you are listening, pick out the answers to these questions:
a)  When did the Togolese start changing back to their old ways?
b)  Who do the students visit before their exams?
c)  Why don't the Togolese go to the police?

## 4  Language study

### a)  Vocabulary and pronunciation: verb v. noun stress

'Convert' and 'conflict' are two of quite a large set of English words which have the same form for both noun and verb, the difference lying in the stress. The noun is stressed on the first syllable, while the verb is stressed on the second. Here is a list of some of the most common. Write two short sentences for each, one with the word as a verb, the other as a noun. Then practise the correct stress:

eg  They were con*ver*ted to the idea. The evangelist made many *con*verts.

| | |
|---|---|
| combat | compact |
| compound | conflict |
| convict | exploit |
| export | intrigue |
| import | permit |
| process | produce |
| progress | prospect |
| protest | rebel |
| record | reject |

**b)  Useful words and phrases: expressions with 'time'**
The speaker uses several phrases with the word 'time'. Fit the following expressions into the sentences below (use each one once only).

*by the time / on time / from time to time / at the same time / at the time / in no time at all / two at a time / in time*

1  I'm surprised how quickly it happened. It was over _____.
2  The animals went into the ark _____.
3  I visit him _____ but not very often.
4  If we don't hurry it'll have finished _____ we get there.
5  He was wrong, but _____ you shouldn't have lost your temper.
6  Late again! This train's never _____.
7  It couldn't have been me, officer — I was in bed _____.
8  The performance starts at 8.30. I hope we get there _____.

**c)  Language focus: articles**
'The President . . .': We use the definite article when we are sure which one we are referring to (the speaker must mean the President of Togo) or if we have already mentioned the noun. However, we often omit the article with common place names associated with a function. Compare:

He's still at school. (He is a student)
There was a fire at the school.

When we talk generally, we usually omit the article and make countable nouns plural,

eg  Coffee is a popular drink.
Bees make honey.

**d)  Activity**
Fill in the blanks in the following sentences with 'a(n)' or 'the', only where necessary (beware of exceptions!):

1  My brother is _____ captain. He studied _____ navigation at _____ college for three years and then joined _____ navy and went to _____ sea.
2  You needn't stay in _____ class if you feel so ill. Go _____ home and go to _____ bed. I'll call _____ doctor. I hope you won't have to go to _____ hospital.
3  He used to go to _____ church, but now he no longer believes in _____ God, and worships _____ Devil.
4  _____ Earth is nearer _____ Sun than _____ Saturn.
5  _____ elephants have _____ good memory.
6  My sister plays _____ clarinet in _____ orchestra.
7  _____ most of my friends are in _____ prison.
8  I'll meet you outside _____ cinema. We can go for _____ meal in _____ new Chinese restaurant.

9  I like all _____ wine, but I really prefer _____ French wine to any other.

10  I work in _____ bank, but I am studying _____ history in _____ evenings.

# 5  Transfer

## a)  Tape

Each section of this tape deals with one aspect of the Togolese traditional beliefs: protection against evil, medicine, and crime. Here are some of the key words used in each section. Read them through and then listen to the tape again and place them in the correct boxes:

*gourd / fetish / herbs / rope / bad luck / pendant / ritual / curses / psychology / harm / cure / amulet / fee / guilt / disease*

| Protection | Medicine | Crime |
|---|---|---|
|  |  |  |

## b)  Discussion

We might describe some of what the speakers talk about as superstition. In most countries, certain happenings, dates, objects or animals are associated with good luck or bad luck. What are they in your country and do you believe in them?

# 6  Writing

**Write about one of these:**

a)  Describe any traditional remedies used in your country for common ailments.

b)  Modern medicine has a lot to learn from traditional experience.

# MODULE 8
## FOOD A

## 1 Setting the scene

## 2 Vocabulary

| | | |
|---|---|---|
| inhibition *n* | (l.9) | feeling that something shouldn't be done |
| stem from *v phr* | (l.10) | originate from |
| favour *vt* | (l.26) | like |
| slaughter *vt* | (l.31) | kill (animals) for food |
| crawl *vi* | (l.32) | move slowly on one's hands and knees |
| unwary *adj* | (l.34) | careless |
| pitfall *n* | (l.34) | unexpected danger |
| inconsiderate *adj* | (l.39) | not thinking of other people's feelings |
| swill *vt* | (l.40) | drink large quantities of |
| grumble *vi* | (l.42) | complain |

## 3 Text

While reading the text find the answers to the following questions.
a) What three aspects of British life does the writer link in the text?
b) Which class drinks what for breakfast?
c) In what way are upper-class food habits changing today?

# FOOD

*The characters*
Harry Stow-Crat and family — members of the aristocracy
Gideon Upward and family — members of the upper middle class
Mr Bryan and Mrs Jen Teale and family — members of the lower middle class.
5  Mr Definitely-Disgusting and family — members of the working class
Mr Nouveau-Richards and family — a new millionaire

The food you eat often indicates what class you are; the way you eat it, namely
your table manners, does so almost as much. The upper classes, for example,
don't have any middle-class inhibitions about waiting until everyone else is
10  served; they start eating the moment food is out in front of them. This stems
from the days when they all dined at long baronial tables, and if you waited for
fifty other people to be served, your wild boar would be stone cold. Nor would
Harry Stow-Crat comment on the food at a dinner party, because there's no
point in congratulating your hostess on something that's been cooked by some-
15  one else. Equally if he knocked his wine over, he wouldn't apologise, because,
traditionally, there would be a fleet of servants to clean it up.

As one moves through the day, the class indicators come thick and fast. Both
Harry and Gideon Upward would lunch from one o'clock onwards, have tea
around four, and dinner at eight to eight-thirty in the evening. The Teales would
20  breakfast very early because they don't like to be rushed. So would the Definitely-
Disgustings because Mr Definitely-Disgusting has to get to work early. Both
Bryan and Mr Definitely-Disgusting probably have a cheese roll or a bar of
chocolate at nine-thirty, followed by 'dinner' at twelve, and 'tea' the moment
they get home from work about six to six-thirty.

25  The higher classes have coffee for breakfast, the lower have tea, which they
drink very strong and usually sweet. Jen Teale says she doesn't favour either a
'cooked breakfast' or a 'continental breakfast', and instead has 'just a drink in
the morning', meaning tea. (When Gideon Upward or Harry Stow-Crat use the
word 'drink' they mean alcohol.)

30  On to luncheon where gentlemen, according to Harry Stow-Crat, never have
soup — presumably because the upper classes were always out slaughtering
wildlife, and soup would be difficult to eat if you were crawling through the
bracken, or sitting on a horse.

On to tea, which for the unwary is also full of pitfalls. It is very unsmart to call
35  it 'afternoon tea' to distinguish it from 'high tea'. Now that people of all classes
in a hurry use tea bags, everyone puts the milk in second, so there is no longer
any upper-class indicator.

If you stayed with the Stow-Crats you would go into dinner at eight on the
dot, because it's inconsiderate to keep the servants waiting, and you wouldn't sit
40  around the table swilling brandy until midnight, because the servants want to
clear away. But the men would stay behind with the port for a while, and
grumble about estate duty, while the women would go into the drawing-room
and probably moan about constipation.

The worst thing about the working classes, complains Caroline Stow-Crat, is
45  that they never know when to leave. If she asks them round for a quick pre-
dinner drink, they've always had their tea first, and are all set to carry on
drinking until midnight. Samantha Upward gets round the problem by asking
Mrs Nouveau-Richards at seven, then lies that she's frightfully sorry she and
Gideon have got to go out to dinner at eight-thirty.

50  Things are changing, however. These days you find far more upper-class
people complimenting the hostess on her food, because she's probably cooked it
herself — and if you've spent two days slaving over a dinner party you want a bit
of praise. In London fewer and fewer men wear black ties, although the upper
classes and upper middles still tend to in the country, with many of the women
55  still sticking to their horse blanket long skirts and frilly shirts.

*(From* **Class** *by Jilly Cooper)*

# 4  Language study

## a)  Vocabulary

The following verbs indicate either a positive, neutral or negative attitude

Indicate positive with +; indicate negative with –; indicate neutral with N.
The first one has been done for you.

> comment   N
> congratulate
> grumble
> complain
> praise
> say
> compliment
> moan

## b) Useful words and phrases: prepositional and phrasal verbs

Below is a list of phrasal verbs from the text. Match the verb phrase on the left
with the one on the right that has the closest meaning:

| | | | |
|---|---|---|---|
| 1 | knock over | a | invite |
| 2 | clean up | b | make tidy |
| 3 | clear away | c | continue |
| 4 | ask round | d | work hard |
| 5 | carry on | e | spill |
| 6 | slave over | f | refuse to change |
| 7 | stick to | g | remove |

## c)  Language focus: 'would' in conditional II and past habits

Notice how 'would' is used in the following sentences:
1   If you waited for fifty other people to be served, your wild boar would be
stone cold.
2   Both Harry and Gideon Upward would lunch from one o'clock onwards.
In 1 'would' is used in the main clause of a conditional II type sentence.
In 2 'would' is used to indicate a habit or characteristic pattern of behaviour in
the past. This use of 'would' is often found in written narrative, while in speech
'used to' would be more usual.

## d)  Activity

Now rewrite the following sentences using a construction with 'would'. The first
one has been done for you.
1   When I was a child I always used to eat at regular meal times.
    When I was a child I would always eat at regular meal times.

2   Sometimes I didn't arrive home on time and my parents were very angry.
    If _____

3   When I went to university I got into the habit of eating at all times of the day
    and night.

    _____

4   Sometimes I didn't have time for a proper meal. So I survived on snacks.
    If _____

5   But when I was really hungry I used to go home for some real food.

    _____

6   Then I got married. Sometimes I came home late and my wife got furious.
    Then I got married. If _____

7   Then it was my habit to reminisce about the freedom of my university days.

    _____

8   But then I considered everything — I didn't want to change.
    But if _____

102

Now look at Language study Section a) again, and then complete the following text using a verb or derived noun in the gaps. Use each item only once:

'Guess what's for supper', she said. 'Go on.'
'Oh no ..... not sausage and chips again', he (1)_____ as the plate was pushed in front of him.
'The only time you ever (2)_____ on my cooking is when you've got a (3)_____ to make. You can't have caviar and champagne everyday — not on your salary! So stop (4)_____, and get on with it!' 'That's just not true', he (5)_____ in a hurt voice. 'I often (6)_____ you on your cooking, but my (7)_____ always falls on deaf ears ...... OK, I apologise. I (8)_____ you on your preparation of an exquisite English traditional dish!'

# 5 Transfer

### a) Text
Complete the following table by inserting the appropriate name given by each class to each of the meals of the day:

| Class | Name of | | | |
|---|---|---|---|---|
| | 1st meal | 2nd meal | 3rd meal | 4th meal |
| Working | | | | |
| Lower middle | | | | |
| Upper middle | | | | |
| Upper | | | | |

### b) Discussion
To what extent are food, table manners and social class linked in your country?

# 6 Writing

### Write about one of these:
a)   Write a letter to a foreign friend describing a national or regional dish.
b)   Eating good food is one of the greatest pleasures in life.

## 1   Setting the scene

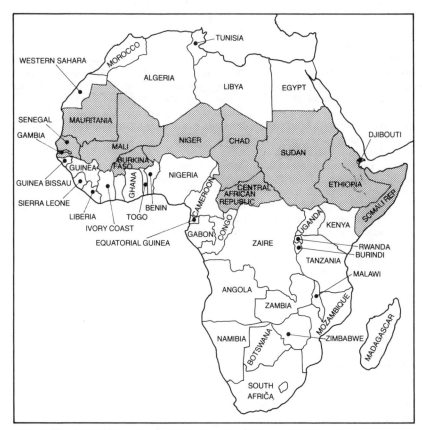

## 2   Vocabulary

| | | |
|---|---|---|
| famine *n* | (l.1) | very serious lack of food |
| drought *n* | (l.9) | very serious lack of water |
| aggravate *vt* | (l.11) | make worse |
| commodities *n pl* | (l.28) | products |
| harvest *n* | (l.38) | amount of crops gathered |
| arid *adj* | (l.44) | very dry |
| accelerate *vt* | (l.46) | make something happen earlier |
| scramble *n* | (l.47) | struggle |
| erosion *n* | (l.51) | action of becoming worn away |
| exacerbate *vt* | (l.58) | make worse |
| short-sightedness *n* | (l.60) | inability to see or think clearly |
| trappings *n pl* | (l.62) | ornamental decorations |

## 3   Text

While reading the text find the answers to the following questions.
a)   Where, according to the writer, do the roots of Africa's starvation lie?
b)   Why does Kenya's government encourage cash-cropping?
c)   What sector of development does the writer claim that many African governments put before agricultural development?

# ■ WHY AFRICA GOES HUNGRY

All of us have seen the famine pictures from Ethiopia and the Sudan. We know people are starving; we've responded generously with food aid. A 'natural disaster' or 'act of God', we tell ourselves, as if the famine has been a freak, one-off event. We assume that when the rains come
5 again, everything will be all right.

But it won't.

The truth is that not just Ethiopians but many millions of Africans, from Mauritania across to Somalia, face starvation. And the underlying cause is *not* drought. The real roots of the famine lie with the people and the way
10 they have used, and abused, the land. The recent drought has simply aggravated what is largely a political and economic problem.

Even in Kenya, one of the more wealthy Black African nations, food shortage is a growing problem. In fact the tragedy that is unfolding in Kenya is typical of what's happening in an estimated 20 other countries on the
15 southern fringes of the Sahara. The popular images of Kenya — lions, avocados, coffee — imply rich grasslands and good farming. But less than 20 per cent of Kenya's land has high or moderate agricultural potential. Even so, there is enough good farmland to meet the nation's growing food needs. So what has gone wrong?

20 One reason is that cash-cropping is increasing. A large proportion of farmland is devoted to coffee, tea, pyrethrum, pineapples and to raising other cash crops in order to earn much-needed foreign exchange on the export market. These cash crops are the backbone of Kenya's economy; tea and coffee alone account for more than half the country's export earnings. They
25 provide employment — in Kenya only about one adult in ten has a regular wage — and pay for Nairobi's impressive development.

But here's the first catch in the story. In the past 15 years, while the cost of tractors, fertilizers and fuel — all imported commodities — has risen sharply, the real value of coffee and tea has fallen. Kenya's lifeline to stability has been
30 threatened. So, to keep up the income from the exports, the government has encouraged yet more cash-cropping.

Tens of thousands of 'shamba' farmers (smallholders) contribute to Kenya's exports by planting coffee. To them it looks, at first, an attractive proposition. A shamba is usually an acre or two in size; typically it grows a
35 mixture of food crops — maize, with some cow peas, beans, bananas — and a cash crop, usually coffee. In a good year the coffee can earn the farmer a few hundred pounds with which he'll pay for clothing and education for his children. But if the world prices fall, or if there's a bad harvest, these farmers suffer.

40 The population explosion in Kenya means that shamba land is bursting at the seams. All the productive land that isn't already growing cash crops has been taken for shambas, which get divided and subdivided among the growing families. When suitable land runs out, the farmers get squeezed out — down to the arid bush country or up to the hill slopes.

45 Hill slopes are cleared of forest to make way for crops, but this only accelerates the crisis. Kenya has already lost half its natural woodland since independence in 1963. There's a desperate scramble for cleared land and for firewood. Almost all Kenyans use wood, or wood charcoal, as a cooking and heating fuel. Everywhere you go, women carry huge bunches of firewood
50 strapped to their backs.

The deforestation has serious consequences. It leads to soil erosion, which was an underlying cause of Ethiopia's famine. Crops of maize are planted on 45-degree slopes without terraces. Within three or four seasons, the topsoil has been washed away by the torrential rains, and the hill is useless for
55 farming.

Another consequence is more subtle. Forests hold on to moisture and are essential creators of rainfall through transpiration. Extensive deforestation may have exacerbated the drought in Africa: fewer forests mean less rainfall, and less rainfall means drought and desertification.

60 In a sense, the problem has arisen because of the short-sightedness of many African governments. They want industrial development and the

trappings of growth and wealth, but they've overlooked the golden rule: development can only take place on a foundation of agricultural surplus. You must feed your people first.

But it would be hypocritical not to lay some of the blame on Western nations ....

*(By Brian Leith, Television Producer with*
*BBC Natural History Unit at Bristol)*

# 4  Language study

## a) Vocabulary: types of land

The following words deal with different types of land. Link the word on the left with its meaning on the right:

| | | | |
|---|---|---|---|
| 1 | grassland | a) | finely powdered earth |
| 2 | woodland | b) | uncleared wild country |
| 3 | farmland | c) | land used for cattle to feed on |
| 4 | bush | d) | area covered with trees |
| 5 | slope | e) | flat, level area cut from a slope |
| 6 | soil | f) | land used for growing crops |
| 7 | dust | g) | piece of ground going up or down |
| 8 | terrace | h) | top covering of the earth |

## b) Useful words and phrases: 'lie, lay, rise, arise', and 'raise'

Look at the following sentences taken from the text that exemplify the use of the above verbs:
— The real roots of the famine lie with the people
— and to raising other cash crops
— while the cost of tractors, fertilizers and fuel has risen sharply
— In a sense, the problem has arisen because of the short-sightedness of many African governments
— But it would be hypocritical not to lay some of the blame on Western nations

Now complete the verb table below:

| Verb | Transitive/ Intransitive | Principal forms | Meaning |
|---|---|---|---|
| arise | I | arose arisen | happen |
| | | | place or put |
| | | | be or remain (horizontal) |
| | | | cause to rise or grow |
| | | | increase |

## c) Language focus: present perfect

Below are two uses of the present perfect with examples taken from the text
1  to describe an event in the indefinite past. Here we are not concerned with when an event happened (in contrast to the definite past):
— all of us have seen ...
— we've responded generously with food aid
2  to describe an event in the definite past which either
a)  continues to the present:
— in the past 15 years the real value of coffee and tea has fallen
or
b)  has a result in the present:
— the recent drought has simply aggravated ...
— all the productive land has been taken for shambas
— Kenya has already lost half its natural woodland

**d) Activity**

Rewrite the following sentences in the present perfect, using a verb form derived from the word in italics. The first one has been done for you.

1 Today we have an oversupply of food in Europe as a *result* of intensive farming.

Today intensive farming has resulted in an oversupply of food in Europe.

2 We have an *accumulation* of butter, milk and meat.

_____

3 European countries regularly hold *discussions* on this matter. These discussions started some years ago.

_____

4 But we have no *solution* to the problem of how to reduce these mountains.

_____

5 A small number of Third World countries receive some of this food as a *gift*.

_____

# 5  Transfer

**a)  Text**

The text presents a number of causes and results which form links in a chain. Complete the following diagram. The symbol ⟶ indicates the relationship between cause and result:

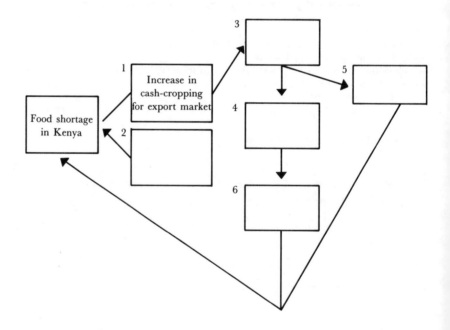

**b)  Discussion**

The text ends 'But it would be hypocritical not to lay some of the blame on Western nations ...' Do you think the West has done enough?

# 6  Writing

**Write about one of these:**

a) Write a letter to a charity organisation suggesting ways in which you would like to see world food problems tackled.

b) We have a duty to feed the hungry.

# I   Setting the scene

| Wholefoods Restaurant | |
|---|---|
| Lentil curry and rice | 2.95 |
| Mushroom quiche and rice | 3.45 |
| Stuffed marrow and rice | 3.60 |

| AI CAFE | |
|---|---|
| Egg and chips | 1.30 |
| Hamburger and chips | 1.75 |
| Sausage and chips | 1.60 |

# 2   Vocabulary

| | |
|---|---|
| refined /rɪˈfaɪnd/ | free from other substances |
| roughage /ˈrʌfɪdʒ/ | coarse matter in food that aids digestion |
| sprinkle on /ˈsprɪŋkəl on/ | put on small quantities |
| bran /bræn/ | crushed skin of wheat and other grain |
| innovation /ɪnəˈveɪʃən/ | introduction of something new |
| additive /ˈædətɪv/ | something added to food |
| nutrient /ˈnjuːtrɪənt/ | healthy elements in food |
| wholemeal bread /ˈhəʊlmiːl bred/ | bread made from all the grain |
| convenience foods /kənˈviːnɪəns fuːdz/ | foods which can be cooked quickly |
| emulsifiers /ɪˈmʌlsɪfaɪəz/ | a chemical that changes a number of liquid ingredients into a semi-solid |
| dose /dəʊs/ | quantity |
| incidence /ˈɪnsɪdəns/ | occurrence |

# 3   Tape

Jo Whitehead is a nutritionist and dietician with varied experience of working with food, both in the catering and medical spheres. In this interview Jo talks about the present British diet, and presents criticisms levelled at it by various health experts.

As you are listening, find the answers to the following questions:

a)   What does the typical working household's diet lack?
b)   Who is the only person that is listened to when it comes to diet?
c)   What are the two changes in diet that Jo has noticed over the last five years?

# 4   Language study

**a)   Vocabulary and pronunciation: adjectives and adverbs**

Here are some adjectives and adverbs taken from the tape. First underline the syllable which carries the main word stress. Then link the word on the left with its definition on the right.

| | | | |
|---|---|---|---|
| 1 | typical | a) | in fact |
| 2 | recent | b) | especially |
| 3 | actually | c) | almost certainly |
| 4 | generally | d) | normal |
| 5 | probably | e) | new |
| 6 | significant | f) | usually |
| 7 | particularly | g) | substantial |

**b) Useful words and phrases: expressions with 'take'**

The speaker uses a number of phrases with 'take'.

| | |
|---|---|
| take-away | take notice (of) |
| take place | take heed (of) |
| take in | take up |

Now complete the following sentences using the above phrases.

1 I believe a change is ——————— in eating habits.

2 More and more people are ——————— what their doctors are saying.

3 They are also ——————— more sports and physical activities.

4 As a result they are ——————— fewer harmful chemicals than they would get at the ———————.

**c) Language focus: cause and effect**

In the dialogue Jo describes the relationship between diet and health, in particular focusing on how a poor diet can cause health problems. This relationship (between cause and effect) can be expressed in a number of different ways. If we represent the relationship diagrammatically it would look as follows:

| A | ⟶ | B |
|---|---|---|
| A poor diet | can cause | ill health |

Here | A | represents the cause.
| → | represents the process (verb).
| B | represents the effect.

1 Verbs and verb phrases indicating the cause/effect process:

| | |
|---|---|
| lead to | give rise to |
| cause | be responsible for |
| results in | account for |
| bring about | |

eg A poor diet can lead to health problems.

2 Adverbial phrases indicating the cause:

| | As a result of | a poor diet, | health problems can arise. |
|---|---|---|---|
| eg | adverbial phrase | A | B |

Other adverbial phrases indicating the cause are:

because of
as a consequence of
due to
owing to
on account of

All of these phrases must be followed by a noun (phrase),
eg Because of a poor diet, health problems can arise.
or Health problems can arise because of a poor diet.

3 Adverbial links

Here we are focusing on a cause in a previous sentence,

| eg | .... a poor diet. | Consequently | health problems can arise. |
|---|---|---|---|
|  | A | adverbial link | B |

Other adverbial links indicating the cause are:

therefore
so
as a consequence
as a result
that's why (informal)

4 We can also view the relationship as B ←————————— A. This is in fact the same as A —————————→ B.

| Health problems | can result from<br>stem from<br>be attributable to | a poor diet. |
|---|---|---|
| B | ←————————— | A—————————→ |

d) Activity

Look at the vicious circle below, and then complete the sentences using the words and clues given. The first one has been done for you.

```
                    ↗  1   unhappiness  ↘

  8  can't find a job                       2   excessive eating
              ↖
     7  sickness                    3  overweight    4  poverty
              ↖                              ↘           ↙
        6  weakness          ←          5  decision to diet
```

1 → 2 (result in)      I've heard that my unhappiness may *result in excessive eating/*.

3 ← 2 (stem from)      But of course it's very likely that ____ may ____
                        _____

2 → 4 (as a result of) And _____ , _____
                        can also arise.

4 → 5                   So I've decided _____

5 → 6 (cause)          But _____ _____

6 → 7 (give rise to)   And this will clearly _____

7 → 8 (due to)         And then _____ , I won't _____

1 ← 8 (result from)    I've heard that _____ may _____
                        not being able _____ !

# 5 Transfer

a) Tape

In the notes below either the cause or the effect is missing. Complete them using the information on the tape.

1 Overcooked vegetables ————————→ loss of _____
2 Realisation of importance of food ←———————— research of
   _____
3 _____ can ————————→ certain diseases.
4 Fried food is likely to ————————→ _____
5 But heart disease also ←———————— _____
6 _____ ————————→ the consumption of more vegetables.

b) Discussion

You are what you eat.

# 6 Writing

**Write about one of these:**

a) People are becoming more diet-conscious.
b) Food should be rationed to ensure that people eat a balanced diet.

# MODULE 8
## FOOD D

## 1 Setting the scene

## 2 Vocabulary

| | |
|---|---|
| exotic /eg'zotɪk/ | strange and unusual |
| ingredient /ɪn'gri:dɪənt/ | one of a mixture of things used in cooking |
| texture /'tekstjə/ | the way something feels to the touch |
| paramount /'pærəmaunt/ | very great |
| soya sauce /'sɔɪjə sɔ:s/ | dark brown liquid made from soya beans |
| mushy /mʌʃɪ/ | overcooked |
| soggy /sogɪ/ | completely wet and soft from overcooking |
| etiquette /etɪ'ket/ | behaviour |
| chopsticks /'tʃopstɪks/ | pair of narrow sticks used for eating |
| seaweed /'si:wi:d/ | plant which grows in the sea |

## 3 Tape

The conversation on the tape takes place in a Japanese restaurant in Tokyo. Tomoko, a Japanese student, is explaining different aspects of Japanese food and eating habits to her English guest.

As you listen, answer the following questions.

a) What three factors are considered of major importance in Japanese food?
b) What are the vegetable dishes cooked in?
c) What foods does Tomoko say have become popular in Japan in this century?

## 4 Language study

### a) Vocabulary: verbs of perception

The verbs of perception, which relate to the five senses, can be classified into:
— link verbs, complementing the subject either with an adjective phrase or a noun phrase,

eg   that sounds interesting
     that sounds (like) an interesting story

— full verbs denoting unintentional sense perception

eg   I heard an interesting story

— full verbs denoting intentional sense perception

eg   I listened to an interesting story

Now complete the following table. Note that the same verb may appear in all three columns:

| Sense | Link verbs | Full verbs/ unintentional | Full verbs/ intentional |
|---|---|---|---|
| sight | | | |
| smell | | | |
| hearing | | | |
| touch | | | |
| taste | | | |

### b) Useful words and phrases: exclamations

1 with 'how'

'how' + adjective: How absolutely delicious! How interesting!

2 with 'what'

'what' + noun: What a spread! What a shame! What a far cry from mushy peas!

Now complete the following exclamations:

1 _____ disgusting!
2 _____ a delicious meal!
3 _____ ridiculous!
4 _____ a stupid thing to do!
5 _____ an absolutely fantastic idea!

### c) Language focus: emphasis

Emphasis is used to colour the attitudes and emotions of speakers to what they say, often in order to influence the attitudes and behaviour of their listeners.

Below are some of the methods that can be used:

### 1 Interjections

Ah, I think this is ours coming now. /ɑː/ — recognition

Ooh, it looks fantastic! /uː/ — pleasure

Mm, how absolutely delicious! — pleasure

Wow, this meal is absolutely fantastic! /waʊ/ — great surprise

Phew, I haven't eaten so much for ages! /fjuː/ — exhaustion

Ugh, what was that!? /ʌx/ — disgust

### 2 Fronted topic

Here another element, instead of the subject, is emphasised by moving it to the front of the sentence. This is a typical feature of informal conversation,

eg  Two major points I would consider important.

 Well, the vegetable dishes they're cooked in soya sauce.

Notice that the fronted element is usually given the nuclear stress, thus doubling the emphasis.

### 3 Inversion

Here not only the topic element, but also the verb phrase, or part of it, is moved before the subject,

eg  Not only must it taste good ....

 Under no circumstances were children allowed to speak at table

 Here comes our meal now

### 4 Cleft sentences

A cleft sentence splits the sentence into two halves, emphasising the topic. This can be done in two ways:

— 'it' + 'be' + 'that' clause (cleft 'it'),

eg  It's soya sauce that helps to preserve the texture

 It's not only traditions that are changing

— 'wh'−word + relative clause + 'be' + 'that' clause (cleft 'wh'),

eg  What I mean is that the food must taste and look good

 What people in the west don't realise is that the ingredients are very similar

### 5 Intensifying adverbs and modifiers

It looks *really* fantastic!

How *absolutely* delicious!

You can't *possibly* achieve the same effect.

It used to be an *extremely* social activity.

It's healthy *indeed*.

**d)  Activity**

**1  Verbs of perception**

Complete the following sentences with an appropriate verb of perception in the correct tense:

a)  What's that music? It _____ familiar.

b)  When I arrived home last night my wife _____ the soup because she thought she'd burnt it.

c)  On my way to work this morning I _____ a terrible accident.

d)  Why _____ that film again? We saw it at the cinema only last week.

e)  I (not) _____ very well. I think I'll go home.

f)  I _____ they're going to open a Japanese restaurant next to the supermarket.

g)  This perfume _____ very exotic.

h)  What are you doing?

   I _____ the clothes to see if they're dry.

**2  Emphasis**

Rewrite the following sentences to emphasise the underlined words, using the word indicated,

eg  Bread was introduced in Japan only recently. (It)

   It was only recently that bread was introduced in Japan.

a)  The food must not only taste good, but it must also look good. (Not only)

b)  The appearance of the food is of paramount importance. (What)

c)  The appearance of the food is of paramount importance. (It)

d)  Bread was introduced in Japan only recently. (only)

e)  It tastes delicious. (How)

f)  That's really a nuisance. (What)

g)  They add soya sauce. (What)

h)  Soya sauce preserves the texture of the food. (It)

# 5  Transfer

**a)  Tape**

Listen to the tape again and at the same time complete the following 'Japanese Food Guide':

| Japanese Food Guide | | |
|---|---|---|
| Purposes of soya sauce | 1 | _____ |
| | 2 | _____ |
| Reasons for changes in Japanese eating habits | 1 | _____ |
| | 2 | _____ |
| Reasons why Japanese food is healthier than western food | 1 | _____ |
| | 2 | _____ |

**b)  Discussion**

Although most people would agree that they eat to live rather than live to eat, obesity and poor diet are still problems in many 'developed' countries. Why do you think that this is the case?

# 6  Writing

**Write about one of these:**

a)  Write a letter to a friend to persuade him/her to become a vegetarian.

b)  A meal can only taste nice if it looks nice.

# I Setting the scene

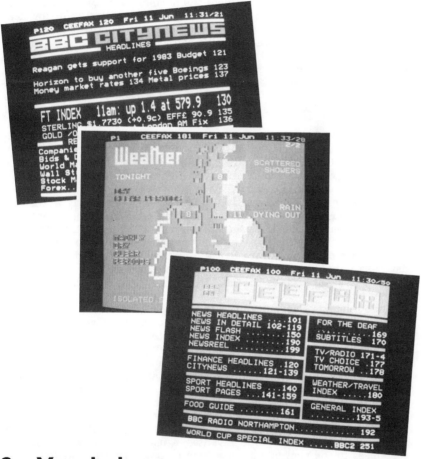

# 2 Vocabulary

|  |  |  |  |
|---|---|---|---|
| supersede | *vt* | (1.1) | replace with something better |
| comprehensive | *adj* | (1.4) | including everything |
| update | *vt* | (1.7) | change or extend with the latest information |
| host | *n* | (1.9) | large number |
| summon | *vt* | (1.9) | call |
| superimpose | *vt* | (1.10) | place on top of |
| graphics | *n* | (1.26) | pictures or diagrams |
| network | *n* | (1.46) | number of systems joined together |
| potential | *adj* | (1.48) | possible in the future |
| recipient | *n* | (1.63) | person who receives |

# 3 Text

While reading the text, find the answers to these questions:
a) What is the main difference between teletext and normal television viewing?
b) In what way are viewdata and teletext different?
c) What is the main use of viewdata at the moment?

# ■ VIEWDATA AND TELETEXT

Just as black and white television has been gradually superseded in most British homes by colour TV, so these in turn are steadily being replaced by sets that have a teletext facility on them. Both ITV and BBC offer a comprehensive service on both of their channels,
5 allowing those viewers with teletext to gain access to a wide variety of information at any time of the day from a centralised bank of information stored on computer and continually updated. This includes travel information, weather forecasts, general, sporting and financial news and a host of other items that are summoned to the screen at the press
10 of a button. They can either replace the normal TV picture or be superimposed on top of it. The latter facility is especially useful for deaf people, since many of the programmes are now subtitled by teletext, enabling the viewer to read what he cannot hear.

There is also a second development which is well on the way to
15 commercial success. It is called viewdata. Teletext is a passive system: it can only receive information. Viewdata, however, is active: the user can receive information from a computer and talk back to it. Both systems use a regular television set that has been modified to receive a special signal.
20 With viewdata, an ordinary television set equipped with a computerised controller can receive information from a computer over telephone lines. Using the controller, a caller can search the memory of a distant computer and the information he desires will be displayed on the screen before him.
25 Teletext, on the other hand, is simply a method of sending words and graphics over the air. The teletext signal rides on the same signal that brings ordinary television programmes into the home. Viewers use a keyboard to choose the pages of information they wish to consult, but the operator cannot talk back to the computer. The whole of the teletext
30 database is broadcast continuously; when a viewer tells the machine which particular page is needed, the computerised controller tunes in to that page.

While teletext is very useful to the householder, viewdata has wider applications, particularly for businesses, because it allows this two-way
35 communication between people and computers. For this reason, in the next few years viewdata will probably continue to attract more users in the office than in the home. It is already in standard use, for example, with travel agents, who can check seat availability on particular flights or trains. To do this, the agent calls up the viewdata service and re-
40 quests the booking information. Using a system called gateway, a seat can then be reserved by typing the necessary details onto the keyboard.

Gateway was the most important development in public viewdata. In the early days, before it was invented, a user could only give simple responses to the viewdata services' main computer, whereas today the
45 public system user can be linked to a private computer. Thus the travel agent, for instance, goes through the viewdata network to an airline's computer, which answers questions through a public system.

The potential uses of gateway are many. Already some banks are giving viewdata terminals to their customers so that they can carry out
50 their transactions from home. In the not-too-distant future you may well be able to go teleshopping from your armchair by ordering goods from local stores on credit and having them delivered as well — a particularly useful service for the elderly and disabled.

Alongside the public viewdata system, there are also many private
55 systems already in use. Some very large companies with vast stores of information now prefer a system of their own rather than sharing on a public one. With a private system a company uses its own computer to provide clients or employees with information such as prices and supplies, company accounts, or holiday dates. Both public and private view-
60 data networks are also used for sending post electronically. The message to be sent is typed on a screen and the number of the person to receive it is dialled in just the same way as on a telephone. The electro-

nic message is stored in a 'postbox' in the computer and the recipient is told that there is a letter which can be read either immediately or left until later when the television set is on. And it is not only text that can be transmitted in this way. Diagrams, photographs and virtually any other type of graphic information can also be sent electronically from one machine to another anywhere in the world. Perhaps the postman's days are numbered.

*(From **Discovering Communications** by J Stanstell)*

# 4 Language study

### a) Vocabulary: technical language

The passage uses a number of technical words or phrases to do with TV and computers. Use these words or phrases in the right place in the text:

*displayed / keyboard / network / broadcast / tunes in / database / linked / transmitted / subtitled*

The whole of the teletext (1)_____ is (2)_____ together with the television signal, and a user simply (3)_____ to the page he wants. The information is then (4)_____ on his screen. Some programmes are (5)_____ so that deaf people can read what is being said. Viewdata users, on the other hand, have a (6)_____ on which they can type messages to be (7)_____ to a central computer which is (8)_____ to the (9)_____.

### b) Useful words and phrases: word families

Complete the following table of word families:

| Verb | Agent | Action/concept | Adjective |
|------|-------|----------------|-----------|
|  | informant |  |  |
| receive |  |  |  |
|  | — |  | normal |
| reserve | — |  |  |
|  |  |  | modified |
| communicate |  |  |  |
|  |  |  | employed |
| prefer | — |  |  |
| transmit |  |  | — |
| broadcast |  |  | — |

### c) Language focus: punctuation: the comma, the colon and the semi-colon

The passage uses the comma, the semi-colon and the colon in a fairly typical way, although the rules for their use in English are not very precise. The comma, especially, has no hard-and-fast rules, but it is used generally to make reading easier. A good principle to follow is to use commas whenever the normal English pattern of Subject-Verb-Object-Adverbial is interrupted.

The colon is a simpler matter: it goes between independent clauses where the second explains or fulfils the first, or before a list.

The semi-colon usually replaces 'and' with two independent clauses; it is used in more formal writing.

### d) Activity

Punctuate the following sentences:

1 Having made so many mistakes he did however have the grace to apologise.
2 Mr Blake has announced the decision there are to be three new appointments.

3   They decided unwisely in my opinion to continue they hope to finish by Thursday.
4   Luckily we discovered the problem within minutes there was no petrol left.
5   Personally I can only assume one thing he is lying.
6   If he had known he would have come in in spite of the cold.
7   He heard a long slow pulsating beat coming from behind the door he knew he had found it.
8   Whatever else you bring you must carry at least three things a sleeping bag an anorak and a pair of strong boots.
9   The government has in one respect escaped lightly that is there will be no prosecutions.
10  They did incidentally pay for the broken door windows and furniture.
11  James on the other hand disagrees entirely he thinks that they the losers should buy the first round.
12  What he does does not concern us we have more important things to consider.

# 5   Transfer

### a)  Text

Reread the text and decide whether the following statements are true or false:
1   In England, only BBC offers teletext.
2   Only those viewers with a special teletext TV can receive teletext information.
3   You can see both the TV picture and the teletext information at the same time.
4   Viewdata uses a voice system.
5   You can only receive teletext when TV programmes are being broadcast.
6   At the moment, viewdata is more popular in business than in the home.
7   Viewdata is a private system.
8   Viewdata is used by disabled people for shopping.
9   Some large companies use private systems to keep records of staff holiday times.
10  Electronic messages must be read immediately.

### b)  Discussion

Technology is changing our way of life rapidly. Do you think that it improves the quality of our lives or just makes us lazy? Is much of it very useful or just novel?

# 6   Writing

**Write about one of these:**
a)   Describe the way in which technology has changed your life.
b)   We must accept the dangers of nuclear energy as the price of progress.

# 1    Setting the scene

*The Thames Barrier — London's answer to the danger of tidal flooding*

# 2    Vocabulary

| | | |
|---|---|---|
| alarmist *n* | (1.16) | a person who worries about dangers |
| fossil fuels *n phr* | (1.17) | fuels such as oil, coal used for energy |
| lag *n* | (1.31) | delay |
| divert *vt* | (1.40) | change the direction of |
| aquifer *n* | (1.53) | water-bearing rock |
| dyke *n* | (1.68) | protective wall |
| moot *vt* | (1.71) | suggest |
| shrink *vi* | (1.80) | get smaller |
| shelve *vt* | (1.95) | abandon until later |
| snag *n* | (1.109) | difficulty, problem |

# 3    Text

While reading the text, find the answers to these questions:
a)   In what way has man so far slowed the rise of the sea?
b)   What are the other methods suggested?
c)   Which of them seems the most practical?

118

# ■ ROLLING BACK THE WAVES

Throughout this century, the weather has grown erratically warmer. At the same time, the sea level has been rising, also erratically, at an average rate of more than one millimetre a year. The two developments are connected. Not only does water expand when warmed, but a warmer climate makes glaciers melt faster, returning to the sea moisture that has remained locked into ice caps for generations.

A millimetre a year may not sound much, but a rising sea level ought to worry Dutchmen and others who live near low-lying coasts. If the alarmists are right, man's habit of burning fossil fuels to make 'greenhouse' (ie heat-trapping) gases is steadily raising the temperature of the atmosphere, then the sea level could rise three metres by the year 2100.

However, the human race need not get its feet wet. Two American scientists have recently published an ingenious analysis of how to lower the sea level by building reservoirs and flooding depressions in the earth's surface. They calculate that the reservoirs man has built since 1932 have caused a 26-year lag in the rising sea level.

Their arithmetic goes thus: the sea level has risen by 1.25mm or 300 cubic miles a year since 1932. The 107 largest reservoirs in the world hold, altogether, nearly 2000 cubic miles of water.

Small reservoirs probably hold as much again. Irrigation projects have diverted water that would normally go back to the sea into dry soil at the rate of about 80 cubic miles a year, or 4400 cubic miles altogether. That makes 8000 cubic miles of water now on land that would otherwise be in the sea, or 32.5mm of potential sea level rise.

Of course, this is rough and ready arithmetic. Other factors should be taken into account. More reservoirs mean more evaporation, and so more rain, some of which gets into the sea. Much of the water extracted from underground aquifers such as the great Ogalla aquifer on which many Texas farmers depend now finds its way to the sea; it never did before. A warmer climate might make more snow fall than melt in Antarctica, locking up more ice.

None the less, by building reservoirs and irrigation schemes, man has already cancelled out nearly half the rise of the sea level he would otherwise have caused. With a little effort, say the two scientists, he could keep the sea level steady for a good few decades yet. Only then would he have to start building dykes or evacuating coastal cities.

Several big schemes have been mooted that would help lower the sea level. The biggest and most practical is the long-debated Russian scheme to divert parts of three great Siberian rivers that between them carry 1000 cubic miles of water away into the Arctic Ocean each year, south into the Aral and Caspian Seas. The Caspian could do with some water. It is nearly 30 metres below sea level and shrinking all the time. Raising it 10 metres would store 2750 cubic miles of water or eight years' worth of sea rise. The Aral Sea is all but dry.

The aim of the Russian scheme is not, of course, to stop Holland sinking beneath the waves. It is to open up desert for farming with the river water. But that is not going to happen, for the time being at least. The cost and a Gorbachevian distrust of vast engineering projects, plus ecological concerns at the possible effect on the Arctic have combined to persuade the Russian government to shelve it.

Then there are the earth's depressions. Five of them — the Imperial Valley in California, the Qattara Depression in Egypt, the Dead Sea, the Salina Gaulicho of Argentina and the Danakil Depression in Ethiopia — are big enough to hold more than 600 cubic miles each and close enough to the sea to be flooded with seawater. The Israelis have long thought of generating hydroelectric power from Mediterranean water coursing downhill through a tunnel into the Dead Sea. The snag, as so often with these schemes, is that this threatens to disturb the ecological balance and to lose local people their land. And people made landless are not any happier when they are told that shallow inland seas often provide fertile fishing grounds.

*(From The Economist, 12–18 April 1986)*

# 4 Language study


## a) Vocabulary: 'rise' v. 'raise'

The passage uses the two verbs, 'rise' and 'raise' several times. These verbs are often confused in English. 'To rise' is intransitive, that is, it does not take an object (eg 'The sea level has risen') 'To raise' is transitive and takes an object (eg 'The Russians want to raise the level of the Caspian Sea'). 'Arise' is like 'rise' but is more formal and used with non-physical concepts. What are the respective opposites of 'rise' and 'raise'?

A further confusion is caused by a difference in use between British and American English. When an American wants more money he asks for 'a raise'; a British person asks for 'a rise'. Choose between 'rise' and 'raise' and put the correct form in the following sentences:

1 If you know the answer please _____ your hand.
2 It rained all day and the river _____ to a dangerous level.
3 There has been a steady _____ in the cost of living.
4 You are doing very well, but I don't want to _____ your hopes unduly.
5 A problem _____ which will delay things by a day or so.
6 The company plans to _____ the necessary capital through the banks.

## b) Useful words and phrases

Link the phrases on the left, taken from the passage, with phrases of similar meaning on the right:

1 may not sound much     a) approximate
2 as much again     b) nearly
3 rough and ready     c) for the moment
4 none the less     d) does not seem important
5 a good few     e) the same amount
6 could do with     f) nevertheless
7 all but     g) several
8 for the time being     h) needs

## c) Language focus: present perfect v. past

In order to use a past tense the speakers must share (either explicitly or implicitly) a common time reference,
ie 'The sea level rose' has little meaning unless we know when it happened.
This passage talks about a present and possible future situation, with several references to the past. These are in the present perfect tense, because they refer to events which have happened in the past (and may be still happening today), and it is the results of the actions which are important, not the time of their occurrence,
eg 'Two scientists have recently published ...' (l.24) — we can read it now.
'The sea level ... has been rising' (l.3) — the sea level is now higher.

## d) Activity

As a technical expert, you have been asked to draft a report on the present state of a hydroelectric power station. It is now December. Rewrite the following sentences so that they refer to the present situation, using a present perfect:
The first one has been done for you.

1 The power station came on stream six months ago.
  The power station has been on stream for six months. _____

2 It started generating electricity some while ago.

_____

3 Technical problems occurred from the very beginning.

_____

4 Cracks were discovered in the dam wall in March and April.

_____

MODULE 9 TECHNOLOGY B

120

5   The number two turbine ceased operating in June.

6   As a result of industrial mismanagement, the unions withdrew their good-will in August.

7   Environmentalists began demonstrating in September.

8   The Ministry inspectors arrived on the site two months ago.

9   A high level of salinity was detected in the water in November and December.

10  The General Manager resigned yesterday.

# 5   Transfer

**a)   Text**

From your reading of the text, choose the best answers to the following:

1   The sea level this century has risen
    a)   dramatically.                      b)   by a regular amount.
    c)   at a variable rate.                d)   insignificantly.

2   This rise has been slowed by
    a)   burning fossil fuels.              b)   Dutchmen building dykes.
    c)   flooding depressions.              d)   building reservoirs.

3   Texas farming activities have probably
    a)   raised the level slightly.         b)   lowered the level slightly.
    c)   made no difference.                d)   made all the difference.

4   In the Antarctic, a warmer climate may
    a)   melt more ice.                     b)   increase the ice.
    c)   prevent ice from melting.          d)   reduce the snowfall.

5   The Russian plan would transfer water from
    a)   the Arctic.                        b)   the Caspian.
    c)   the South.                         d)   Siberia.

6   How many reasons does the text give for abandoning the Soviet plan?
    a)   One.                               b)   Two.
    c)   Three.                             d)   Not stated.

7   Depressions are
    a)   flooded areas.                     b)   areas below sea level.
    c)   areas with poor economy.           d)   dry areas.

8   The Israeli plan
    a)   is already in operation.           b)   is popular with the local people.
    c)   will improve the ecology.          d)   is not a new idea.

**b)   Discussion**

Has the rise in the sea level affected your country? Have there been any other climatic changes? If so, were they caused by man, and can we do anything about them?

# 6   Writing

**Write about one of these:**

(a)   How far is human activity responsible for changes in our environment?
(b)   Describe a natural disaster which has occurred in your country.

## 1 Setting the scene

## 2 Vocabulary

| | | |
|---|---|---|
| churn out | /tʃə:n aut/ | produce in large amounts |
| store | /stɔ:/ | keep for future reference |
| monitor | /ˈmonɪtə/ | display screen for word processor |
| hard copy | /hɑ:d kopɪ/ | copy on paper |
| load | /ləud/ | transfer information from disc to computer |
| shift | /ʃɪft/ | move |
| save | /seɪv/ | store information on disc |
| bleep | /bli:p/ | short electronic sound |
| carriage return | /ˈkærɪdʒ rɪtə:n/ | movement of typewriter typing position to the next line |
| dig around | /dɪg əˈraund/ | search |
| files | /faɪlz/ | places to store information |
| delete | /dɪˈli:t/ | take away, remove |
| power cut | /ˈpauə kʌt/ | loss of electric power |

## 3 Tape

On this tape, you will hear two people talking about word processors. As you listen to them, find the answers to the following questions:
a)   What does the woman think is the main advantage of the word processor?
b)   How does it compare with a typewriter for ease of operation?
c)   What would be lost in a power cut?

## 4 Language study

### a)  Vocabulary and pronunciation: verbs describing sounds

The tape talks about the 'clacking of keys and the whirring of the carriage return'. We have a wide range of verbs to describe sounds in English. Can you associate the sound verb on the left with the source on the right? Then make up a

122

short sentence to practise the pronunciation of the verbs. (How many of them sound like the noise they represent?)

| | | | |
|---|---|---|---|
| 1 | clatter | a) | an electric motor |
| 2 | hiss | b) | distant thunder |
| 3 | creak | c) | falling glass |
| 4 | thud | d) | water going down a drain |
| 5 | rattle | e) | a rusty door |
| 6 | hum | f) | escaping steam |
| 7 | sizzle | g) | sausages in hot fat |
| 8 | rumble | h) | knives and forks on a plate |
| 9 | gurgle | i) | a body falling to the ground |
| 10 | tinkle | j) | a window in a strong wind |

**b)  Useful words and phrases: expressions with 'far'**
The girl says 'Far from it' — meaning the same as 'Not at all'. The word 'far' has a number of uses in English:
— as an intensifier in expressions like *far too many / far more difficult*
— as an adverb in expressions like *by far / go too far / as far as I know / far removed from / far be it from me*
— as an adjective in expressions such as *a far cry from / on the far side*
And remember that we don't normally use it in positive statements when we mean distant. In response to the question 'How far?', we say 'Not far' or 'A long way.' Fit one of the above expressions into these sentences:
1   I can't possibly carry all these parcels — there are _____.
2   _____ to criticise, but don't you think your skirt is rather short?
3   He's moved to a new house _____ of the town.
4   I've seen all the James Bond films, but this last one is _____ the best.
5   Mr Jones is away _____, but you can call him just to make sure.
6   International trade today is _____ the simple exchanges of the Middle Ages.
7   This exercise is _____ than I imagined.
8   You always _____. Now you'll have to apologise.

**c)  Language focus: genitive forms**
In addition to the general rules given in Module 10C, here are two further points on genitive use.
1   The double genitive. In phrases such as 'this one of ours', English uses 'of' followed by the possessive pronoun, as in the table below:

| Object form | Possessive pronoun |
|---|---|
| me | mine |
| you | yours |
| him | his |
| her | hers |
| us | ours |
| they | theirs |

Where a noun is used, it takes the genitive 's,
eg   An invention of Marconi's

2   The genitive 's (singular only) is also used with names of trades or professions to indicate their place of work,
eg   I must go to the greengrocer's / dentist's this week.
3   There are also a number of common idiomatic phrases using the genitive 's' which may be exceptions to the general rules of genitive usage. Some are given in the exercise below.

**d)  Activity**
Fill in the gaps in the sentences with a genitive, using each of the following words once, or a suitable possessive pronoun:

*arm / pound / wit / doctor / Shakespeare / stone / chemist / moment /*
*harm / water / money / God /*

1   His new house is only a _____ throw from his office.
2   He couldn't think what to do next — he was at his _____ end.
3   A four-course meal with wine and coffee for only £5? You really get your _____ worth.
4   I'll just pop out to the _____ and get some aspirins.
5   He was never very friendly with the staff. He always kept them at _____ length.
6   For _____ sake stop annoying me.
7   If you refuse to help me you are no friend of _____.
8   Hamlet is a famous tragedy of _____.
9   Don't worry at all about it. You mustn't give it a _____ thought.
10  They insisted on bringing a relative of _____ even though non-members were not invited.
11  You look pretty ill to me. Hadn't you better go to the _____?
12  The grandchildren are coming. We must put those precious vases out of _____ way.
13  That cheese is rather expensive. Just give me a _____ worth.
14  He can't swim, so he just stood at the _____ edge and watched.
15  She said he was only a colleague of _____, but they seemed very friendly.

# 5   Transfer

## a)   Tape
Listen again to the tape and answer the following:

**Section I** — fill in the missing word from the dialogue:
1   The word processor has _____ the typewriter in the office.
2   Memory is the word processor's chief _____.
3   A word processor means she doesn't have to _____ with a rubber.

**Section II** — Choose the best answer:
1   The printer
   a)   makes no noise.                b)   is less noisy than a typewriter.
   c)   is traditionally noisy.        d)   is noisier than a typewriter.

2   To print a letter she must
   a)   fill the screen.               b)   check it on the screen.
   c)   press a key.                   d)   quote a reference.

3   A word processor
   a)   can help to dig.               b)   does the digging.
   c)   spends a lot of time digging.  d)   avoids having to use files.

**Section III** — true or false?
1   The speaker's system can store twenty letters per disk.
2   Letters are stored on the screen.
3   Power cuts are a serious problem.

## b)   Discussion
Computers, robots and new electronic machines are gradually taking over many jobs in the world. Is this entirely a good thing, or should it be limited? Could things get out of control?

# 6   Writing

**Write about one of these:**
a)   Describe the way in which computers have affected your life.
b)   Computers can never replace people.

# MODULE 9
## TECHNOLOGY D

## 1 Setting the scene

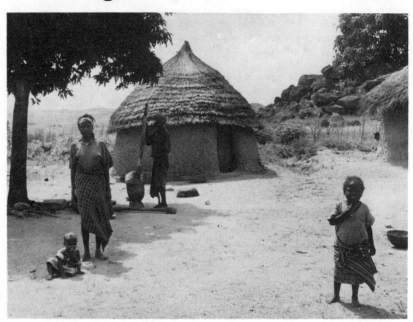

## 2 Vocabulary

| | | |
|---|---|---|
| bursting with | /ˈbɜːstɪŋ wɪð/ | full of |
| spare | /speə/ | extra, not being used |
| cynical | /ˈsɪnɪkl/ | seeing no good in others |
| recycle | /rɪˈsaɪkl/ | use again |
| surplus | /ˈsɜːpləs/ | extra, not needed |
| granaries | /ˈɡrænərɪz/ | places to store grain |
| stilts | /stɪlts/ | poles to raise something above the ground |
| foreign exchange | /forən ɪksˈtʃeɪndʒ/ | foreign currency, other countries' money |
| went bust | /went bʌst/ | failed, became bankrupt |
| syphon | /ˈsaɪfən/ | drawing a liquid by atmospheric pressure |
| hose | /həuz/ | rubber pipe |

## 3 Tape

On this tape you will hear a Senegalese man discussing technology aid for his country with a UN aid worker. As you listen, pick out the answers to the following questions:

a) Why do African countries find it difficult to finance new projects?
b) What were the two problems concerning the American grain stores?
c) What major change did the new manager of the sugar-cane scheme make?

## 4 Language study

### a) Vocabulary and pronunciation

Fill in the table below, underlining the stressed syllable in each word:

| Concept | Adjective | Agent |
|---------|-----------|-------|
| finance | financial | financier |
| | | technologist |
| | beneficial | |
| cynicism | | |
| | | traditionalist |
| extremism | | |
| | operational | |
| | | merchant |
| circumstance | | — |

## b) Useful words and phrases: phrasal verbs

The speaker says that the money goes to 'pay off' their debts. We often use a particle to reinforce the verb in this way. Choose the best particle to reinforce the verbs in the following sentences. The first one has been done for you.

1  He owes me a lot of money, but he won't pay it _____ back _____.
2  I must cut _____ on my smoking.
3  The new machinery has speeded _____ the operations.
4  The shop closed _____ last year.
5  Would the last person to leave please lock _____?
6  It's quite a big stream at the moment, but it dries _____ in the summer.
7  You're soaked to the skin. Sit by the fire and dry _____.
8  If he doesn't slow _____, he's going to be exhausted.
9  My daughter wants to be a nurse when she grows _____.
10 The grandfather clock has run _____. Could you wind it _____ for me?

## c) Language focus: expressing agreement and disagreement

The two speakers do not entirely accept each other's point of view. Here are some of the expressions they used together with others:

| agreement | disagreement |
|-----------|--------------|
| I entirely agree | I totally disagree |
| I couldn't agree more | I can't accept that |
| You're absolutely right | That's completely wrong |
| True | Come on! |
| I accept that | Nonsense! |
| Maybe | Rubbish! |

The choice of expression will depend on the strength of agreement and the heat of the argument. There are, of course, many stronger words of disagreement!

## d) Activity

Below is a jumbled dialogue between two people, A and B, about aid to developing countries. The first statement is given. Rewrite the dialogue in a logical sequence:

A: Well, I know that the gap between the industrialised nations and the Third World is getting bigger all the time. . . .

B: Nonsense! You can't blame that on the industrialised nations too.

B: Now there I disagree. They're not entirely responsible; the Third World countries could do more for themselves.

B: That's just not true. A lot of it is spent by the local governments on projects in the country.

B: I accept that, but who's to blame?

126

B: Maybe you're right. A lot of it does. But how much is wasted through mismanagement and corruption?

B: Come on! They receive millions in aid every year....

A: Do you really think so? That only accounts for a drop in the ocean; most of it goes straight back on expensive technology.

A: The industrialised nations, of course. It's all their fault.

A: Too much, I agree. But that's just bad habits left over from the colonial days.

A: How could they? They're sucked dry by the industrialised nations.

A: True, but what happens to it? It's all paid straight back via the multinationals.

# 5 Transfer

### a) Tape
Listen again to the tape and find the answers to the following:

### Section I
Are these statements true or false according to the speakers?
1 The World Bank prefers to invest in projects costing less than $2m.
2 The Third World countries cannot invest because they owe so much money.
3 The US AID grain stores in Senegal have been a great success.

### Section II
Choose the best answer:
1 The sugar plantation was built to
   a) provide cheap sugar.        b) save on foreign exchange.
   c) provide work locally.        d) compete with the West Indies.
2 The new machinery in the plantation did not work because
   a) it rusted.                b) it broke down immediately.
   c) no-one was trained to use it.   d) the workers refused to use it.
3 The new manager
   a) reduced the workforce.      b) required all the machines.
   c) replaced the machines with  d) employed only single people.
      people.
4 The plantation now uses
   a) no technology at all.       b) all the latest technology.
   c) only syphon technology.    d) the most appropriate technology.

### Section III
Find the missing word:
1 The Dutchman thinks that using lasers is going from one _____ to the other.
2 The laser does the work in a _____ of the time.
3 If there is no new technology, not much _____ is required.
4 The Senegalese speaker felt that the Dutchman's last remark was _____.

### b) Discussion
Modern technology is often offered as the best way to development, but there is a growing movement in favour of more 'appropriate' technology, both in developing countries and the industrialised world. Do you agree that the latest and best technology is not always the best solution? Can you think of examples of inappropriate technology in your country?

# 6 Writing

### Write about one of these:
a) Describe a situation in your country where technology has made a great contribution to the quality of life.
b) 'Small is beautiful.' Discuss this viewpoint with regard to the development of technology.

## 1  Setting the scene

## 2  Vocabulary

| | | |
|---|---|---|
| watercress *n* | (l.3) | plant grown in water, often eaten in salads |
| shawl *n* | (l.9) | piece of cloth worn over a woman's head or shoulders |
| mud *n* | (l.21) | very wet earth |
| sewer *n* | (l.21) | pipe under the ground for carrying water and waste material |
| condescension *n* | (l.30) | showing a feeling of superiority |
| stock *adj* | (l.69) | standard |
| framework *n* | (l.73) | plan, system |
| Workhouse *n* | (l.75) | in former times a place where the poor lived when they were unemployed |
| squirearchy *n* | (l.79) | class of country landowners |
| feckless *adj* | (l.91) | not showing proper responsibility about one's life, money etc |

## 3  Text

While reading the text find the answers to the following questions:

a)  Whom did Mayhew's findings surprise?

b)  What, according to Mayhew, were the two factors responsible for the condition of the poor?

c)  Who do you think 'squandered their own advantages while they scorned the achievements of the poor'?

128

# ■ MAYHEW'S LONDON

A hundred and twenty years ago Henry Mayhew described a watercress seller. She was eight years old, but had lost all childish ways. She told him of her life.

'When the snow is on the ground there's no cresses. I bears the cold — you must; so I puts my hands under my shawl, though it hurts them to take hold of the cresses, especially when we takes 'em to the pump to wash 'em. No: I never see any children crying — it's no use.'

Mayhew was a journalist who explored the streets and slums of London. He talked to beggars and pickpockets; chimney-sweeps and showmen; dockers and gamblers. He met mudlarks — children who lived, or existed, on what they could find in the Thames mud at low tide; and sewer hunters, who crawled up the sewers for what could be got from there. He reveals lives that astonish us today. They astonished the middle-class readers of *The Morning Post* quite as much; in fortnightly articles he showed them the lives of the London poor.

He did it without condescension, without exaggeration, pulling no punches. He was a sober, conscientious journalist, and a brilliant one. He saw miseries to terrify, but he found good things as well: theatres and street-shows and, amid horrors, the astonishing survival of the human spirit.

London in the 1850s was an exploding city. A generation before it had been a town, scarcely reaching Oxford Street. Then agricultural depression, growing population and the new railways brought the same uncheckable expansion that has caused Calcutta, Bombay and Mexico City to double and redouble their population inside ten years. And as in those cities, the newcomers camped in slums and shanty-towns without water or drains; appallingly overcrowded; and desperate. Mayhew described the living that could be made — just — by collecting and re-selling the dog-ends of cigars. London was a city where people could, and did, starve to death.

Mayhew believed it did not have to be like that. He knew that the respectable were not born better, and did not work harder, than the poor. It was lack of opportunity, and lack of education, that divided them. Many of the people he wrote about achieved a dignity unsuspected by his readership. Yet others did not, and were so degraded by hardship as to be hardly human.

Extreme urban poverty on the scale he found was something quite new. It was too new a problem to have a solution. Today's stock responses — slum clearance, new towns, high-rise living — have all been pretty disastrous; then they had not even been thought of. Even the framework for those thoughts did not exist. The standard belief was in Charity and the Workhouse, and even Charity was dangerous. These Victorians were living in an industrial age but thinking as a rural squirearchy. Mayhew brought it home to them that the nineteenth century had caught up.

He did his share of charitable work, but knew it was no sort of answer. His hope was in education and he kept his worst anger for those who squandered their own advantages while they scorned the achievements of the poor.

Those ideas are the standard liberal fare of today. Then they were new. Before Mayhew it was possible to believe that the poor were idle and feckless and had only themselves to blame. After him it was not. He showed Victorians the country they lived in, and the lives of some of the people who made England rich.

Mayhew was born in the same year as Charles Dickens. They wrote on the same themes; but where Dickens used melodrama to rouse a nation's conscience, Mayhew stuck to fact. His water-cress girl, his chimney-sweepers, his five-year-old crossing-sweepers are dogged truth. The Death of Little Nell set thousands weeping. Mayhew had no need for Little Nell. He was Dickens for real.

*(From **New Internationalist**, February 1986)*

# 4 Language study

## a) Vocabulary: environmental conditions

The text deals with environmental conditions — both physical and personal — that the poor had to endure. Match the environmental conditions below with their definitions.

| | | | |
|---|---|---|---|
| 1 | slum | a) | with too many people |
| 2 | shanty-town | b) | difficult conditions of life |
| 3 | high-rise | c) | a city area with dirty and inadequate living conditions |
| 4 | depression | | |
| 5 | overcrowded | d) | a period of reduced business activity |
| 6 | desperate | e) | great unhappiness |
| 7 | hardship | f) | an area with badly-built huts and houses |
| 8 | misery | g) | brought down in the opinions of others |
| 9 | degraded | h) | blocks of flats with several floors |
| 10 | disastrous | i) | extremely unsuccessful |
| | | j) | hopeless |

## b) Useful words and phrases: expressions concerning truth

The following expressions from the text indicate that the writer (or speaker) is being truthful and not exaggerating.
Complete the phrases:

1  to ＿＿＿＿＿＿＿ no punches
2  without ＿＿＿＿＿＿＿
3  to ＿＿＿＿＿＿＿ to fact
4  to ＿＿＿＿＿＿＿ the truth
5  ＿＿＿＿＿＿＿ real

## c) Language focus: linking constructions

Grammar provides three main ways of linking clauses together:

1  Co-ordination with a conjunction, eg 'and,' 'or,' 'but,' etc:
— 'but had lost all childish ways.'
— 'but he found good things as well.'
— 'and did not work harder.'
Notice that the subject can be omitted after co-ordinating conjunctions if it is the same as the subject in the previous clause.

2  Subordination with a conjunction, eg when, though, because, etc:
— 'though it hurts to take hold of the cresses.'
— 'especially when we take 'em to the pump.'
— 'while they scorned the achievements of the poor.'

3  Adverbial link. Here the clauses are separated either by a full-stop(.) or a semi-colon (;), and connected by an adverbial,
eg  so, yet, then, etc:
— 'I bears the cold — you must; so I puts my hands under my shawl.' (1.7)
— 'unsuspected by his readership; Yet others did not, and were so . . . .' (1.62)
— 'Then agricultural depression, growing population and . . . .' (1.41)

Effects of the different linking strategies
1  Co-ordination
Looser connection than the others. Therefore more vague and less emphatic.
2  Subordination
Reduces the subordinated clause to a less important role.
3  Adverbial link
Typical in longer stretches of language to indicate the relationships between sentences and ideas.

The three linking methods mentioned above can be used to express the same basic idea. The effect, however, is different:
She was eight years old, but had lost her all childish ways.
Although she was (only) eight years old, she had lost all childish ways.
She was eight years old; yet she had lost all childish ways.

130

**d) Activity**

Rewrite the following sentences using the type of linking construction indicated in brackets. The first one has been done for you.

1 When the snow is on the ground there's no cresses. (adverbial)
  The snow is on the ground; then there's no cresses.

2 He saw miseries to terrify, but he found good things as well. (adverbial)

3 They camped in slums and shanty towns. There they lived in appalling conditions. (subordinating)

4 The standard belief was in Charity and the Workhouse. Moreover even Charity was dangerous. (co-ordinating)

5 These Victorians were living in an industrial age, but were thinking as a rural squirearchy. (subordinating)

6 Dickens used melodrama to rouse a nation's conscience. In contrast Mayhew stuck to fact. (subordinating)

7 Although the poverty was depressing, it did not destroy the spirit. (co-ordinating)

8 The people supported each other emotionally and physically. So they survived. (subordinating)

9 At that time one had money; alternatively one had friends. (co-ordinating)

10 Mayhew is of interest today because he describes the realities of Victorian England. (adverbial)

# 5 Transfer

**a) Text**

Complete the table below about Mayhew's London:

| Mayhew's London |
| --- |
| Mayhew's profession: _____ |
| Date of study: _____ |
| Where data collected: _____ |
| Social class of readers: _____ |
| Causes of London's problems: 1 _____ |
| 2 _____ |
| Available solutions to      3 _____ |
| problems:              1 _____ |
| 2 _____ |
| Mayhew's famous contemporary: _____ |

**b) Discussion**

Equality of opportunity may exist in principle, but there will always be the more fortunate, the more privileged and the more successful.

# 6 Writing

**Write about one of these:**

a) Write a letter to a friend describing your home and its location.
b) Is the modern world a nice place to live in?

## 1  Setting the scene

## 2  Vocabulary

| | | |
|---|---|---|
| swelter *vi* | (1.1) | to be very hot |
| swarm *vi* | (1.4) | to move in a large crowd |
| outstrip *vt* | (1.23) | to be greater than |
| engulf *vt* | (1.31) | to destroy |
| appalling *adj* | (1.46) | very bad |
| confront *vt* | (1.50) | to face |
| swell *vi* | (1.59) | to grow to a large size |
| stem *vt* | (1.65) | to stop |
| offset *vt* | (1.82) | to balance |
| smog *n* | (1.98) | mixture of smoke and fog |

## 3  Text

While reading the text, find the answers to the following questions:

a)  What two types of problems are expected as a result of the growth of cities over the next twenty years?

b)  What are the three 'solutions' seen by the pessimists to the problem of uncontrolled city growth?

c)  Which places mentioned in the article have made a contribution to improving urban conditions for their inhabitants?

# ■ NIGHTMARE OF THE MONSTER CITIES

It is a sweltering afternoon in the year 2000, in the biggest city ever seen on earth. Twenty-eight million people swarm about an 80-mile-wide mass of smoky slums, surrounding high-rise islands of power and wealth. One third of the city's workforce is unemployed and many of the poor have never seen the city centre. And from the parched countryside a thousand more hungry peasants a day pour into what they think is their city of hope.

That nightmare of the not-too-distant future could be Cairo or Jakarta or any of a dozen other urban monsters. Already Mexico City, São Paulo and Shanghai are among the largest, most congested cities on earth. Over the next two decades, they — and many others — are expected almost to double in size, generating economic and social problems that will far outstrip all previous experience.

Just 30 years ago some 700 million people lived in cities. Today the number stands at 1800 million, and by the end of the century it will top 3000 million — more than half the world's estimated population.

The flood of 'urbanites' is engulfing not the richest countries, but the poorest. By the year 2000 an estimated 650 million people will crowd into 60 cities of five million or more — three-quarters of them in the developing world.

In places where rates of natural population increase exceed three per cent annually — meaning much of the Third World — that alone is enough to double a city's population within 20 years. But equally powerful are the streams of hopeful immigrants from the countryside. More often than not, even the most appalling urban living conditions are an improvement on whatever these people have left behind.

The problem that confronts urban planners is that there have never been cities of 30 million people, let alone ones dependent on roads, sewers and water supplies barely adequate for urban areas a tenth that size.

In contrast to the great urban industrial booms of the nineteenth and twentieth centuries, the flood of new arrivals to today's swelling Third World cities far outstrips the supply of jobs — particularly as modern industries put a premium on technology rather than manpower.

Optimists maintain that runaway urban growth can be stemmed by making rural and small-town life more attractive. Some say that the trend is self-correcting, since conditions will eventually get bad enough to convince people that city life is no improvement after all. But pessimists see a gloomier correction: epidemics, starvation and revolution. In the end, both sides agree that the world's biggest cities are mushrooming into the unknown.

According to an international study, up to a population of half a million, a typical city's employment steadily improves and living conditions remain stable. When the million mark is reached, further improvements in jobs begin to be offset by a decline in the quality of life. Beyond two million inhabitants, only real incomes show a slight rise, with no sizeable improvement in employment conditions and a deterioration of general living conditions in such areas as crime and housing.

Yet some cities still manage to cope. Seoul, riding the crest of South Korea's economic boom, is currently building a £2,500 million underground railway system that should ease some of the worst traffic problems in the world. Over the last decade Tokyo has cleared up much of its legendary smog. Hong Kong has rehoused 1.3 million people in new high-rise towns which are totally self-contained, down to playgrounds, industrial areas and a railway line into the colony's main business district.

The essence of the larger problem is that every step taken to improve living conditions in the slums only attracts more immigrants. One solution is to ban migration into the cities. Both China and the Soviet Union use internal passports or residence permits to try to control urban growth. Moscow has also taken advantage of its state-controlled economy to direct industry, and therefore jobs, to smaller satellite cities or even wholly new urban areas. Tanzania rounds up the unemployed in its cities and transports them to state-run farms.

Such steps — along with population control and measures to improve conditions in the countryside — are today being promoted in much of the Third World. But in a time of widespread economic stagnation, they will not 25 stem the flood.

With the future in mind, Mexico City planners are already laying plans for a metropolitan region of 36 million people by the year 2000. If nothing else, there is a kind of New World bravery 130 in that.

*(From Newsweek, 31 October 1983; article by S. Reiss)*

# 4 Language study

### a) Vocabulary

Complete the following word table:

| Noun | Verb | Adjective |
|---|---|---|
| starvation revolution deterioration stagnation | | |
| | — | gloomy |
| | — | unemployed |

### b) Useful words and phrases: increase and decrease in quantity and quality

The following words indicate either increase or decrease.
Put a ↗ if the word indicates an increase; put a ↘ if the word indicates a decrease

    growth
    mushroom
    deterioration
    decline
    improve
    rise
    boom
    swell

### c) Language focus: present simple and present continuous

The main uses of the present simple are:
1  to describe a truth or current belief,
eg  Up to a population of half a million a typical city's employment steadily improves.
    When the million mark is reached, further improvements ...
2  to describe a habitual or general action,
eg  28 million people swarm about an 80-mile-wide mass of smoky slums.

The main use of the present continuous is:
1  to describe an action happening at the same time as the writer/speaker is writing/speaking,
eg  Seoul is currently building a £2,500 million .....
    Such measures are today being promoted in much of the Third World.
    Mexico City planners are already laying plans for a .......

### d) Activity

Put the verbs in brackets into the correct present tense (simple or continuous, active or passive):
Many people (believe) (1)_____ that greater control (need) (2)_____ to limit the growth of many Third World cities. At present ways of limiting growth (consider) (3)_____ by planners all over the the world. But the problem (grow) (4)_____. Large numbers of unemployed (flock) (5)_____ to the cities every day. One planner recently said: 'We (face) (6)_____ one of the greatest challenges of our time. If we (not act) (7)_____ now, many of our cities will become

unmanageable.' There are many who (agree) (8)_____ with him. But for the poor who (look) (9)_____ for jobs, the cities (seem) (10)_____ to offer the best solution.

# 5 Transfer

**a) Text**

1 Complete the urban population statistics in the table below:

| Urban Population Statistics | | |
|---|---|---|
| **When?** | **Where?** | **How many?** |
| 30 years ago | world total | |
| today | world total | |
| year 2000 | world total | |
| year 2000 | sixty major cities | |
| year 2000 | Mexico city | |

2 Now use the symbols below to indicate the trends in living conditions associated with population size:

↗ improve → remain stable ↘ deteriorate

| **Population** | **Living conditions** |
|---|---|
| up to 0.5 million<br>1 million<br>more than 2 million | |

**b) Discussion**

What measures do you think should be taken to control urban growth?

# 6 Writing

**Write about one of these:**

a) Write a letter to a newspaper on an environmental issue that you feel strongly about.

b) Urban growth must be controlled. What measures would you suggest?

# MODULE 10
## ENVIRONMENT C

## 1  Setting the scene

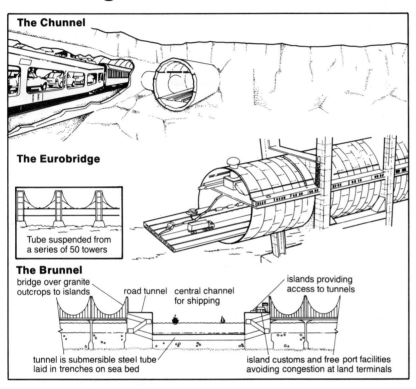

**The Chunnel**

**The Eurobridge**

Tube suspended from
a series of 50 towers

**The Brunnel**

bridge over granite
outcrops to islands — road tunnel — central channel
for shipping — islands providing
access to tunnels

tunnel is submersible steel tube
laid in trenches on sea bed

island customs and free port facilities
avoiding congestion at land terminals

## 2  Vocabulary

hassle /ˈhæsəl/ — annoying difficulties
ferry /ˈferɪ/ — boat that goes across a narrow stretch of water
adjust /əˈdʒʌst/ — change
disembark /dɪsəmˈbɑːk/ — get off a boat
isolation /aɪsəˈleɪʃən/ — state of being separated
differentiate /dɪfəˈrenʃɪeɪt/ — make a difference
rabies /reɪbiːz/ — disease passed on by the bite of an infected animal
vigilance /ˈvɪdʒɪləns/ — continual attentiveness
epidemic /epɪˈdemɪk/ — infectious disease
smuggle /ˈsmʌgəl/ — take from one country to another illegally

## 3  Tape

The building of the Channel tunnel — a rail link between England and the continent — has been a subject of much discussion. On the tape John and Frank debate the advantages and disadvantages of going ahead with the project. While listening to their discussion, answer the following questions.

a)  According to John, who supports the building of the tunnel, what two types of isolation will be reduced?

b)  What two problems is Frank, the opponent of the tunnel, concerned about?

c)  What, according to John, will increase in the long run so that the national economy will benefit?

136

# 4 Language study

## a) Vocabulary and pronunciation

The words below on the left are taken from the tape. First underline the syllable that carries the main word stress. Then match each word on the left with its opposite on the right:

| | | | |
|---|---|---|---|
| 1 | drawback | a) | failure |
| 2 | negative | b) | wasteful |
| 3 | entrance | c) | hell |
| 4 | extinction | d) | positive |
| 5 | efficient | e) | advantage |
| 6 | saving | f) | waste |
| 7 | success | g) | exit |
| 8 | paradise | h) | survival |

## b) Useful words and phrases: phrasal verbs

Check that you understand the meaning of the phrasal verbs below, and then complete the sentences:

> press ahead
> lose out
> be put off
> get to
> look at

If you __(1)_____ the distance between London and Paris, it's ridiculous that there's so much opposition to providing a transport system which will cut travelling time in half. With the tunnel you'll be able to __(2)_____ Paris in just over three hours.

If we don't __(3)_____ with the project we'll be left out of Europe in the long run. And our business community will __(4)_____. So don't __(5)_____ by the arguments that we'll be exposing Britain to new dangers. They're just not true.

## c) Language focus: genitive meanings

The meanings of the genitive, using the apostrophe (') or a construction with 'of', are summarised in the following table. On the left are expressions taken from the tape. On the right are analogous meanings which present the relationship expressed by the expressions.

1 **possessive genitive**
   — Britain's role      Britain has a role
   — the government's policy      the government has a policy
   — the entrance of the tunnel      the tunnel has an entrance
2 **subjective genitive**
   — the spread of rabies      rabies spreads
   — the opening of the tunnel      the tunnel will open
   — the government's decision      the government has decided
3 **objective genitive**
   — the construction of the tunnel      ... will construct the tunnel
   — the development of an efficient transport system      ... will develop an efficient ...
4 **genitive of origin**
   — readers' letters      readers have written letters
   — a source of income      the income comes from a source
5 **partitive genitive and genitive of measure**
   — a part of Europe      Europe is divisible into parts
   — 20 miles of water      the water is 20 miles wide
   — 5 years' work      the work will last 5 years
6 **appositive genitive**
   — the county of Kent      Kent is a county
7 **descriptive genitive**
   — a smugglers' paradise      a paradise for smugglers
   — today's newspaper      the newspaper printed today

The genitive using the apostrophe is typically used in the following cases:
a)  human nouns, eg John's car
b)  animal nouns, eg dog's paws
c)  time nouns, eg today's newspaper
d)  location nouns (especially countries), eg Britain's role (but not with the partitive use, ie the parts of Britain, not Britain's parts)

In other cases the 'of' genitive is normally used.

### d)  Activity
Combine the following nouns with a genitive construction. Remember that if you use an apostrophe, you will need to reverse the order of the words,
eg  newspaper ..... today   today's newspaper
1   the development .... science
2   the future .... Britain
3   a part .... the country
4   the North .... England
5   the decision .... the cabinet
6   the countries .... Europe
7   the creation .... jobs
8   the programme .... next week
9   the history .... the country
10  the brains .... a sheep

# 5  Transfer

### a)  Tape
Now listen to the tape again. While you are listening complete the following summary table about the Channel tunnel:

| The Channel Tunnel | |
| --- | --- |
| Advantages of tunnel system | 1 _____ |
| | 2 _____ |
| Present travel time from London to Paris by rail and ferry | _____ |
| Expected travel time by tunnel rail | _____ |
| Key problem for customs officers when tunnel operational | _____ |
| Man-years of work created by tunnel construction project | _____ |
| Location of entrance to tunnel | _____ |
| Three other areas where jobs will be created | 1 _____ |
| | 2 _____ |
| | 3 _____ |

### b)  Discussion
Many British people say that we already have a ferry link and an air link to the continent, so why build a channel link? Do you support or oppose this view?

# 6  Writing

### Write about one of these:
a)  Describe an eventful journey.
b)  Mass communication has brought the countries of the world closer together.

# MODULE 10
## ENVIRONMENT D

## 1 Setting the scene

## 2 Vocabulary

| | | |
|---|---|---|
| sangria | /sæŋˈgriːə/ | cold drink made from red wine, fruit juice and soda water or lemonade |
| be synonymous with | /biː sɪˈnonɪməs wɪð/ | correspond to |
| flock | /flok/ | go in large numbers |
| pump | /pʌmp/ | provide a lot of |
| shield | /ʃiːld/ | protect |
| mould | /məuld/ | form |
| nubile | /ˈnjuːbaɪl/ | young and sexually attractive |
| dormant | /ˈdɔːmənt/ | asleep |
| galvanise into action | /ˈgælvənaɪz ɪntə ˈækʃən/ | shock into action |
| infrastructure | /ˈɪnfrəstrʌktʃə/ | system which supports an organisation |

## 3 Tape

Spain is Europe's most popular summer holiday destination. In this conversation Ana Maria talks about the development of tourism in Spain and the effects that it has had and is having on the country.

While listening to the conversation, answer the following questions:
a) When did the tourist industry start in Spain?
b) Where did the first tourists come from?
c) Which two countries are competitors to Spain in the tourist market?

# 4 Language study

### a) Vocabulary and pronunciation

The words below on the left are taken from the tape. First underline the syllable that carries the main word stress. Then match each word on the left with its opposite on the right.

| | | | |
|---|---|---|---|
| 1 | isolated | a) | progressive |
| 2 | conservative | b) | ugly |
| 3 | backward | c) | domestic |
| 4 | dormant | d) | truthfulness |
| 5 | attractive | e) | liberal |
| 6 | foreign | f) | open |
| 7 | hypocrisy | g) | slight |
| 8 | radical | h) | awake |

### b) Useful words and phrases

The following adverbs from the tape show the commitment of the speaker to the truthfulness of what is said:

*obviously / certainly / undoubtedly / clearly / plainly*

Rewrite the following sentences so that they have the same meaning as the sentence given. The first one has been done for you.

1 He obviously knows what he is doing.
   It is obvious (that) he knows what he is doing. _____

2 It is certain that he is at home by now.
   He _____.

3 It is undoubtedly a serious mistake.
   There _____.

4 It is clear that he is dishonest.
   He _____.

5 He is plainly bored.
   It _____.

### c) Language focus: addition and exception

#### 1 Addition

The following phrases taken from the tape show how addition is expressed:
— the average tourist isn't looking for anything *besides* that.
— and then there's the Balearics, *as well*.
— and the Canaries, *too*.
— the tourists do go to other places *in addition to* the costas.
— and, *what's more*, with a strong Catholic tradition
— the Church was undoubtedly *also* galvanised into action
— I think ... *So do I*.
— I don't think ... *Nor do I*.

#### 2 Exception

The following phrases taken from the tape show how exception is expressed:
— Spain has a lot to offer *apart from* sun, sand and sangria
— *except for* the coast and the islands, the country hasn't been too greatly affected
— *otherwise*, I don't think there are other countries with .....
— they don't do anything *but* lie on the beach

**d) Activity**

Combine the sentence part on the left with the most appropriate part on the right:

1  Tourism brings in money
2  Tourists often don't want anything
3  Social attitudes have changed
4  The tourist industry isn't booming
5  The bars and restaurants are beginning to suffer
6  Many small businesses will go bankrupt

a)  but a cheap and cheerful holiday.
b)  apart from in the coastal regions.
c)  and shops, too.
d)  except for the well-established ones.
e)  in addition to religious practices.
f)  as well as creating jobs.

# Transfer

**a) Tape**

Complete the following table of information about the development of Spain's tourist industry:

| | |
|---|---|
| Objectives of average tourist to Spain | 1 _____ |
| | 2 _____ |
| | 3 _____ |
| Location of mainland tourist resorts | _____ and _____ |
| High-season months | _____ and _____ |
| Three types of change caused by tourism | 1 _____ |
| | 2 _____ |
| | 3 _____ |
| Initial reaction to first northern European tourists | _____ |
| Finance for tourism provided by | _____ |
| Service industries likely to suffer from reduced tourist spending in the future | 1 _____ |
| | 2 _____ |
| | 3 _____ |

**b) Discussion**

Tourism broadens the horizons.

# 6  Writing

**Write about one of these:**

a)  Write a letter to a friend describing a popular tourist centre in your country.
b)  The tourist industry helps people from different countries make contact and understand each other better. Discuss.

## 1  Setting the scene

*Mr Walker's office*

## 2  Vocabulary

| | | |
|---|---|---|
| split *vt* | (1.8) | divide |
| handy *adj* | (1.9) | convenient, close |
| nanny *n* | (1.18) | private children's nurse |
| moan *vi* | (1.33) | complain |
| barrage *n* | (1.35) | continuous attack |
| press cuttings *n phr* | (1.42) | articles cut from newspapers to keep |
| erupt *vi* | (1.59) | explode violently (like a volcano) |
| surgery *n* | (1.68) | meetings with local people |
| placid *adj* | (1.97) | calm |
| impetuous *adj* | (1.100) | acting without thought |
| recess *n* | (1.103) | parliamentary holiday |

## 3  Text

While reading the text, find the answers to these questions:
a)  What job does the writer have?
b)  Approximately how long does he normally spend at work every day?
c)  What does he do to relax?

# ■ A LIFE IN THE DAY OF PETER WALKER

When you are in politics as head of a ministry you never stop working. It's not like a factory or an office job where you do
5 your 40 hours and go home. One never really stops. But if you enjoy it as I do, then it's not work at all.

I lead a split life between our home in Westminster — it's very handy,
10 just next door to the House of Commons — and our home in Droitwich, Worcestershire.

The family is always together, that's one of our rules. Wherever one
15 of us has to be, we all are.

Tessa and I are getting pretty expert at looking after children. We've never had a nanny but the children are getting older now and lending a hand. If
20 you were to ask the children which house is home they would say both.

On a working day I'm usually up at 6.30 am, although it's certainly not to have breakfast. I don't even have a
25 cup of tea. I call the children at 6.45. They always have a cooked breakfast and I do the cooking, except at the weekends when the children like to make breakfast.
30 Then I glance through the papers but I seldom see any breakfast TV. The children see a bit of it but if I'm ever on they moan like mad. There's normally a race to switch it off or a
35 barrage of witty hostile remarks.

After breakfast I normally do the school run. The children go to different schools but they're all nearby, so I deliver them, then go straight on to
40 the ministry.

The first thing I do is to read a summary of all that day's press cuttings relating to my department. I catch up with the newspapers
45 throughout the day.

Then I meet with the ministers of my department to discuss any important matters. There's six of us and we spend about 20 minutes together.
50 After that I move into a routine of other meetings.

I enjoy the House of Commons very much, even after nearly 25 years. I still get a thrill when I go there.
55 It's quite beyond prediction. You're speaking during a debate and the whole House is quiet, people bored stiff with your speech. Then suddenly the place erupts.

I frequently lunch in my office — 60 often it's a working lunch. If I'm not in the Commons I spend the rest of the afternoon in my office working — and then I usually leave around 6 pm. I always try to get home then as that's 65 when the children have their supper.

On Saturday mornings I usually hold my surgery in Worcester. With five children it can be a bit of a bore giving up Saturday mornings, but it's 70 something I think important for a politician. It makes him realise that all the things he thinks important are not really the things which are worrying people. 75

On average I see 20 people each Saturday, so that means each week I have another 20 cases to take up on their behalf. Some evenings I have to attend dinners and make after-dinner 80 speeches, but it's something I usually enjoy.

At some stage during the day, often during the evening, I make time for an hour's meditation. I sit in an arm- 85 chair, perhaps with a glass of whisky, and consider what's happened during the day and what's going to happen tomorrow. I think of what the importance of it all is. I think of family 90 things.

What it does is to put life into perspective. Something which at 10 am seemed a terrible worry is no longer a worry when viewed in the context of 95 what life is all about. That's why I think I am a placid person. For some people a small event can become an obsession. Meditation stops one being constantly impetuous and in politics 100 that's important.

We always spend the parliamentary recess in Droitwich so the children can get the best of both worlds, living in a great capital city and in the coun- 105 try. I never think of myself as a town or country person, I seem to fit into both worlds.

I never worry about what the future holds in politics. I take things as they 110 come, otherwise there's too much to worry about.

First you worry about becoming an MP; then you worry about becoming a minister of state; then you worry 115 about becoming secretary of state, chancellor, foreign secretary or prime minister. And when you reach any of

those positions you worry about losing them. If you are crazy enough to do that you will not enjoy politics.

*(From* **Sunday, Times Magazine,** *15 December 1986; article by Bill Kellon)*

# 4 Language study

## a) Vocabulary

The writer works in politics. He is a politician. Complete the following table:

| politics | politician |
|----------|------------|
| mathematics | |
| physics | |
| | dentist |
| architecture | |
| | accountant |
| beauty | |
| sculpture | |
| | banker |
| | engineer |
| surgery | |
| | nurse |
| law | |

## b) Useful words and phrases: abbreviations

The speaker is an MP (Member of Parliament); he will normally use these letters after his name. What do the following common abbreviations stand for?

1 After people's names:

| PM | OBE |
|----|-----|
| PhD | BSc |
| QC | JP |
| VC | GM |

2 In written English:

| eg | ie |
|----|-----|
| op cit | sic |
| cf | qv |
| PTO | RSVP |

3 British organisations:

| BBC | TUC |
|-----|-----|
| YHA | C of E |
| CID | RAF |
| VSO | NHS |
| IBA | RN |
| RSPCA | NSPCC |

4 International organisations:

| WHO | UNO |
|-----|-----|
| UNICEF | UNESCO |
| NATO | EEC |
| FAO | IMF |

5 Miscellaneous British:

| PAYE | VAT |
|------|-----|
| GMT | BST |
| PC | SRN |

## c) Language focus: position of adverbials

The passage describes the daily life of a politician, using many adverbials of time and frequency. There are quite strict rules about the position of such adverbials in the English sentence. Although you may find exceptions, it is wise to stick to the standard formula, keeping the adverbials before the subject or after the object, never between the verb and the object:

| Adverbial of time/ place | S | Modal/ Auxiliary | Adverb of frequency | V | O | Adverbial of place | Adverbial of time |
|---|---|---|---|---|---|---|---|
| On Saturday | I<br>I | can<br>would | normally<br>normally | read<br>hold | reports<br>my surgery | in Worcester | after lunch<br>after lunch |

**d) Activity**
Use the following prompts to make up sentences: The first one has been done for you.

1 touch — Mr Jones — since 1944 — alcohol — never
   Mr Jones has never touched alcohol since 1944.

2 shop — early — always — should — you — on Fridays

3 occasionally — can — the cuckoo — hear — in April

4 on holiday — generally — most English people — in August — go

5 hippies — can — you — see — in the 60's — in the streets — often

# 5  Transfer

**a) Text**
From the information in the text, and making some assumptions, fill in the writer's diary for a typical day (use note form):

| | |
|---|---|
| 6.30 am | |
| | |
| | |
| | |
| | |
| | |
| | |
| 6 pm | |

**b) Discussion**
The writer seems to have found a happy balance between his family responsibilities and his career. Which is generally more important in your country — family commitments or job? How do you feel about it personally?

# 6  Writing

**Write about one of these:**
a) If you were a politician, what would be the most important changes you would like to see in your society?
b) Describe a typical day in your life.

# 1 Setting the scene

# 2 Vocabulary

| | | |
|---|---|---|
| laundress *v* | (1.2) | woman who washes clothes |
| confiscate *vt* | (1.5) | take without payment or permission |
| rummage *vi* | (1.8) | search thoroughly |
| discard *vt* | (1.9) | throw away |
| matriculation *n* | (1.12) | getting the right qualifications to enter university |
| caddy *vi* | (1.15) | carry golf equipment for a player |
| stint *n* | (1.30) | fixed amount or period of work |
| blistering *adj* | (1.33) | very strong and sharp |
| wrath *n* | (1.34) | anger |
| stay aloof *v phr* | (1.61) | keep away |

# 3 Text

During your reading of the text, find the answers to the following questions:
a) Why did Desmond Tutu give up his career as a teacher?
b) What was his government's attitude when he won the Nobel prize?
c) Why does he disclaim any political ambitions?

# ■ BISHOP TUTU

**B**orn on the West Rand in 1932 of a Motswana mother who worked as a laundress and a Xhosa father who taught at the local school, Desmond Mpilo Tutu's tribally mixed parentage caused problems with the bureaucrats of the tribal homelands system set up under apartheid. In his passport,

5 which was confiscated frequently as punishment for his criticism, his nationality was described as 'undetermined at present'. This is apartheid's 'final solution', he noted. Tutu could remember as a child his black schoolmates venturing on to the grounds of a white school to rummage through dustbins into which the white children had discarded their unwanted school lunches. At senior school

10 near Johannesburg the young Tutu came under the influence of a white priest, Trevor Huddleston, a major figure in the early years of the anti-apartheid struggle. On matriculation, he was accepted by the medical faculty of the University of Witwatersrand, but lack of funds meant that he could not take up his place. Instead he spent three years at the all-black 'Bantu Normal College' in

15 Pretoria reading for his BA. To make a little spending money, Tutu caddied at the local white golf course, but admitted he didn't have much of an eye for lost balls.

For four years after graduation, Tutu taught at secondary schools, in the process meeting and marrying his wife, Leah, another teacher. But in 1957 the

20 Bantu Education Act was passed and he objected strongly to having to work in the new system which was designed to restrict black education to a level consistent with primary forms of labour.

It was then, at the age of 25, that Tutu joined the Church. After attending theological college in Johannesburg, he left for England, where he studied

25 divinity at King's College, London, before returning in 1962 to lecture on theology in South Africa and Lesotho. Three years later, he went back to London with his wife and four children to work for the World Council of Churches.

In 1975, Tutu became the first black dean at Johannesburg Cathedral, going

30 from there, after a short stint as Bishop of the Diocese of Lesotho, to take up the hot seat as general secretary of the South African Council of Churches, the official spokesman for the country's 13 million Christians. It was a controversial appointment, and he soon used the Council as a launching pad for blistering attacks on apartheid. It was not long before the wrath of the administration

35 descended upon him, and in 1981 a commission was set up to investigate the affairs of the Council.

In an eloquent submission, Tutu attacked the all-white commission for seeing things from a white perspective. In a voice of extraordinary range — from booming bass to angry yelp — Tutu attacked his accusers. He warned them

40 that they were 'taking on the Church of God'; and that other tyrants before them had tried to destroy the Church — Nero, Amin, Hitler, Bokassa. 'Where are they today? They have bitten the dust ignominiously. I warn the South African government again — they are not gods, they are merely mortals who will end up as mere marks on the pages of history, part of its flotsam and

45 jetsam. I am not afraid of them.'

When he was awarded the Nobel Peace Prize in 1984, after having been nominated twice before, the government reaction was foreseeable. While Tutu accepted the prize on behalf of 'all those people whose noses are rubbed into the dust every day', and blacks were jubilant, the government issued a terse 'no

50 comment', and the Afrikaans press fulminated that the late Alfred Nobel would be turning in his grave. Polls were conducted to show that three-quarters of white people in South Africa believed he did not deserve the award.

In 1986, he was appointed Archbishop of Capetown — head of the Anglican Church in South Africa. Many observers saw this irrepressible imp of a man

55 who liked to describe himself as a teddy bear, as the only figure holding back a tide of violence against the state.

A reluctant leader, who admitted to being 'catapulted into prominence' because all the black political leaders were in prison or exiled, Tutu dismissed any suggestion of personal political ambition. He cited three good reasons

60 against this: Archbishop Makarios, Ayatollah Khomeini and Bishop Muzorewa. Instead, he tried to stay aloof from the partisan black politics, reserving his

SLEGS BLANKES
WHITES ONLY

energy for attacking apartheid, and he remained a popular figure with a wide range of black political groupings.

*(From 'Tutu on a Tightrope' by Peter Godwin,*
**Sunday Times Magazine,** *8 June 1986)*

# 4 Language study

## a) Vocabulary: occupations
Desmond Tutu had a variety of jobs, each with a title associated with it. Link the title on the left with the location associated with it on the right:

| | | | |
|---|---|---|---|
| 1 | dean | a) | night club |
| 2 | bishop | b) | bank |
| 3 | headmaster | c) | aeroplane |
| 4 | director | d) | diocese |
| 5 | clerk | e) | court |
| 6 | foreman | f) | kitchen |
| 7 | barrister | g) | cathedral |
| 8 | vicar | h) | company |
| 9 | bouncer | i) | school |
| 10 | receptionist | j) | church |
| 11 | stewardess | k) | building site |
| 12 | chef | l) | hotel |

## b) Useful words and phrases: images and metaphors
The passage contains many colourful images and metaphors:
1 the hot seat (l.31)
2 a launching pad (l.33)
3 bite the dust (l.42)
4 flotsam and jetsam (l.44)
5 irrepressible imp (l.54)
6 teddy bear (l.55)
7 holding back a tide of ... (l.55)
8 catapulted into prominence (l.57)
Match them against their plainer equivalents:
a) suddenly made important
b) discarded rubbish
c) cuddly children's toy
d) preventing
e) the difficult position
f) die
g) starting position
h) lively little devil

## c) Language focus: infinitive 'to' v. preposition 'to'
The word 'to' can be used either as an infinitive particle or as a preposition. Compare the following:
'... a man who liked *to* describe himself as a teddy bear'
'... he objected strongly *to* having to work in the new system ...'

In the first example above, the whole infinitive phrase can be replaced grammatically by a noun or noun phrase:
'... a man who liked his freedom.'
   In the second, because it is a preposition, it must be followed by a noun or noun phrase or the -ing form of the verb:
'... he objected strongly to these measures.'

## d) Activity
Complete the following sentences with the verb given in brackets, adding the correct preposition or infinitive particle where necessary:
1 I was very interested _____ the results of your test; you did well. (learn)
2 I can't say I'm very fond _____ homework. (correct)
3 The boarders are really looking forward _____ for the weekend. (get away)

4   I feel obliged _____ you about your conduct. (warn)
5   I was surprised that David admitted _____ in the exam. (cheat)
6   The sixth form are very interested _____ a newspaper. (start)
7   The new students will soon become accustomed _____ the school rules. (follow)
8   The headmaster was relieved _____ that the keys were not lost. (find)
9   The new maths master must get used _____ with unruly classes. (deal)
10  The housemaster insists _____ everyone at 6 am. (wake)
11  The older students object _____ to play football every week. (have)
12  The games master said he was not prepared _____ laziness. (tolerate)

# 5  Transfer

**a)  Text**

Refer to the text and fill in the milestones in Desmond Tutu's life:

| Date | What? | Where? |
|------|-------|--------|
| 1932 | | |
| 1950 | | |
| 1953 | | |
| 1957 | | |
| 1962 | | |
| 1975 | | |
| 1984 | | |
| 1986 | | |

**b)  Discussion**

Desmond Tutu tried to maintain a distinction between religion and politics. Is this a realistic distinction? Should religious leaders keep out of political life?

# 6  Writing

**Write about one of these:**

a)  Describe the person you most admire in your country.
b)  Who would you nominate for a Nobel Peace Prize, and why?

## 1 Setting the scene

## 2 Vocabulary

| | |
|---|---|
| crops /krops/ | food grown on a farm |
| wheat /wiːt/ | grain crop from which flour is made |
| ploughing /ˈplauɪŋ/ | turning the soil to prepare it |
| subsidies /ˈsʌbsɪdɪz/ | government money given to support farmers |
| harvest /ˈhɑːvɪst/ | gathering the crops from the fields |
| whisked away /ˈwɪskt əˈwei/ | taken away quickly |
| churn /tʃəːn/ | container in which butter is made |
| hay /heɪ/ | dry grass used for animal food |
| barn /bɑːn/ | large building used to store hay |
| folks /fəuks/ | relatives |
| nigh on /naɪ on/ | almost |
| fret /fret/ | worry |

## 3 Tape

The speaker on the tape is a retired farmer talking about the changes he has
seen. While listening to him, find the answers to the following questions:
a) What is the old farmer's complaint about the Ruddock farm today?
b) What does he think the wheat farmer spends most time on?
c) Why does he think people need holidays?

## 4 Language study

**a) Vocabulary and pronunciation: nouns of quantity**
The speaker talks about 'hams' and 'loaves of bread'. We don't often buy a
whole ham, but how often do you buy a loaf? In what quantities do you buy the

150

following? Link the items on the right with their usual packaging on the left, and practise saying them as a phrase with the unstressed /əv/:

| | | | | |
|---|---|---|---|---|
| 1 | a tube | | a) | potatoes |
| 2 | a packet | | b) | cheese |
| 3 | a slice | | c) | toilet paper |
| 4 | a tin | | d) | beer |
| 5 | a box | | e) | strawberries |
| 6 | a jar | | f) | cigarettes |
| 7 | a ball | of | g) | icecream |
| 8 | a bar | | h) | bacon |
| 9 | a can | | i) | matches |
| 10 | a piece | | j) | toothpaste |
| 11 | a punnet | | k) | chocolate |
| 12 | a bag | | l) | baked beans |
| 13 | a tub | | m) | string |
| 14 | a roll | | n) | honey |

**b) Useful words and phrases: time expressions**

Put the following time expressions in the correct columns:

*at the moment / soon / these days / once upon a time / in the immediate future / in recent times / at present / at the time / in olden times / in days to come / presently / in the past / nowadays / in a while*

| Past | Present | Future |
|---|---|---|
| | | |

Choose one of the above expressions to complete the following:

1 _____, there was a beautiful princess who lived in a castle.
2 _____, knights would duel for their lady's honour.
3 I didn't hear the news because I was in New York _____.
4 Could you call later? I'm rather busy _____.
5 _____ there have been many significant advances in the field of medicine.

**c) Language focus: 'used to' v. 'be used to'**

The farmer says that 'Farms aren't what they used to be'.
'Used to' can only be used in the past tense, and is followed by the infinitive. It describes a habitual action or state in the past which is not true now. It contrasts with the present simple.

'Be used to' can be used in the past or present tense, and is followed by the -ing form of the verb or a noun,

eg   The modern farmer is used to filling in forms.

This implies that he knows *how* to do it through experience, but does not necessarily do it regularly.

**d) Activity**

Complete the following sentences with the correct form of 'used to' or 'be used to'; change the verb in brackets to the correct form, where necessary.

1 I have been abroad many times so I (drive) _____ on the right.
2 When I was a boy, I (help) _____ my father on the farm.
3 Farm labourers (work) _____ long hours, even today.
4 As she came from a rich family, she (not do) _____ any housework.

5 As soon as we had collected in the harvest, we (celebrate) _____.
6 In the old days, farming (be) _____ labour intensive.
7 Nowadays cows (be milked) _____ by machine.
8 Farmers never (have) _____ holidays.

# 5 Transfer

## a) Tape

Listen again to the retired farmer and against the list of things below, mark 'O' for 'old' if you think they are things which have disappeared, 'N' for 'new' if you think they did not exist in his day, or 'S' for 'same' if you think they have not changed:

_____ machinery  _____ paperwork  _____ free-range hens
_____ mixed farming  _____ hedges  _____ ploughing
_____ insecticides  _____ subsidies  _____ hams
_____ home-made bread _____ fancy meals  _____ barns
_____ holidays abroad

## b) Discussion

Farming in England is now a highly-mechanised, commercial industry. But many people are worried that the quality of food is not as good as it was, and feel that farmers should now concentrate more on quality than quantity. They feel that people should be willing to pay more for good food. Do you agree, or should the surplus food be given to poor people or countries?

# 6 Writing

**Write about one of these:**

a) Describe the changes that have occurred in farming in your country over the past fifty years.
b) The material quality of life has improved, but the spiritual quality has declined.

# MODULE 11
## PEOPLE D

## 1 Setting the scene

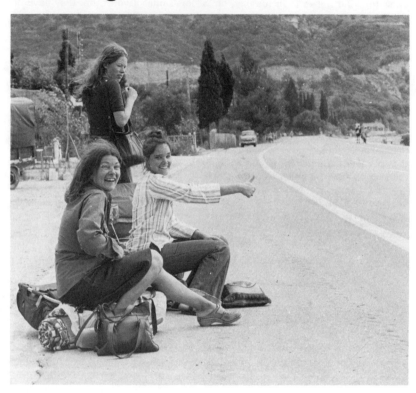

## 2 Vocabulary

| | |
|---|---|
| misconception /mɪskən¦sepʃən/ | wrong idea |
| ex-cons /eks¦kons/ | ex-convicts, former prisoners |
| kids /kɪdz/ | children |
| swig /swɪg/ | drink (slang) |
| Poms /pomz/ | British people (Australian slang) |
| ads /ædz/ | advertisements (short form) |
| lager /¦lɑːgə/ | type of beer |
| infuriate /ɪn¦fjuərɪeɪt/ | make very angry |
| figure /¦fɪgə/ | appear |

## 3 Tape

On this tape, an Australian girl is talking about her trip to Europe. While listening to her, pick out the answers to the following questions:
a)  How did she travel around Europe?
b)  How does she feel in England?
c)  What annoys her most about the English?

## 4 Language study

### a)  Vocabulary: nationalities

The people of Australia are Australians (sometimes called Aussies). They speak English. Fill in the table below for other nationalities:

| Country | Language | People | Adjective |
|---|---|---|---|
| Denmark | | | |
| Brazil | | | |
| | | the Swiss | |
| | | | Belgian |
| | Greek | | |
| Tunisia | | | |
| | | the Bangladeshi | |
| Holland | | | |
| | | | Egyptian |
| Poland | | | |

### b) Useful words and phrases: expressions with 'come'

'All Australians came from here' — this seems an unusual expression, since 'come' is usually associated with motion towards the speaker or the place in question (here), while 'go' is used to suggest motion away from the speaker (there). It is, of course, the specialised use referring to the origin or home of the speaker. (Note: in this sense it is never used in the continuous tense — you would never ask 'Where are you coming from?') The choice of 'go' or 'come' in many sentences depends on the speaker's association of ideas. You can say: 'We're going to the cinema tonight. Would you like to go?' or 'Would you like to come?' In the first case, the speaker is thinking of the place (there), while in the second he is thinking of the people (with us). When you write a letter, you would use 'come' in both the following:

'I am thinking of coming to see you in England next year' (If you are writing to a person in England and thinking of the place the letter is being read) and 'When are you coming to see me?' (You are thinking of the place you are writing the letter).

And then there are the many phrasal verb uses of 'come'. What are the missing particles in these sentences?:

1 He fainted, and came _____ five minutes later.
2 I came _____ some old letters when I was cleaning out the drawer.
3 Come _____ it! You're joking.
4 If we don't come _____ with a solution, we'll have to admit defeat.
5 Arthur won't be here today — he's just come _____ with the flu.
6 You were lucky to get a copy of that book — they're very hard to come _____.
7 He may not agree at the moment, but he'll come _____ to our view sooner or later.
8 We're taking the baby to the doctor because she's come _____ in a rash.
9 When his father died, he came _____ a lot of money.

### c) Language focus: participle constructions

'Australia being so new, we don't have all these ...'. This is a slightly unusual form in spoken English, as we more often give reasons in speech with clauses with 'because', 'since', 'as' etc. But it is quite common in written English to express reason or result with a participle construction, eg:

Having arrived early, John decided to go for a walk.
Wishing to make a good impression, Suzanne wore her best clothes.
Robbed of victory, the team argued lengthily amongst themselves.

But a word of warning: the participle should refer to the subject of the sentence in these constructions, otherwise the relationship may not be clear, eg:

154

Coming from Scotland, people always assume that I should have a Scottish accent.

— Who comes from Scotland?

**d) Activity**

Rewrite the following sentences, using a participle construction as in the examples above (be careful about the subject!) The first one has been done for you.

1 He had made up his mind to leave, so he stood up and looked for the host.
   Having made up his mind to leave, he stood up and looked for the host.

2 As I live in the country, I have to commute to work every day.
   _____

3 Since he had failed his exams, they told David he would have to leave.
   _____

4 Because she was constantly being followed by the press, the young starlet decided to go into hiding.
   _____

5 As he was so shy, he could never pluck up the courage to ask her.
   _____

6 Now that we have discovered the cause of the problem, we must take steps to solve it.
   _____

7 They were curious, so they investigated further.
   _____

8 The company were looking for new investments because they had made such large profits.
   _____

# 5 Transfer

**a) Tape**

Listen to the tape once more and pick out the answers to the following:

**Section I**

Fill in the gaps:

1 Helen's father was _____ her hitch-hiking.
2 She enjoys the _____ of history everywhere.
3 For her, Sydney is a different world _____ Venice or Paris.

**Section II**

1 Because she is Australian, she feels
   a) more at home in England.         b) the same as she did in Paris.
   c) more of a foreigner in            d) more like the English.
      England than Paris.

2 English people expected her to be
   a) short and dark.                   b) tall and dark.
   c) short and blonde.                 d) tall and blonde.

3 She feels that the Englishman's image of Australians is
   a) a joke.                           b) a fair picture.
   c) based on ignorance.               d) based on fact.

**b) Discussion**

Helen feels that English people do not learn enough about the rest of the world, particularly Australia. Is this true in your educational system? Do you think schools should spend more time learning about other cultures and traditions?

# 6 Writing

**Write about one of these:**

a) Describe the worst journey you have ever had.
b) Travelling on foot is the best way of seeing a country.

# MODULE 12
## HEALTH AND MEDICINE A

## 1 Setting the scene

## 2 Vocabulary

| | | |
|---|---|---|
| pressure *n* | (l.13) | condition which causes stress |
| anxiety *n* | (l.14) | stress caused by worry |
| tension *n* | (l.15) | stress |
| addict *n* | (l.29) | person unable to free himself from a harmful habit |
| synchronise *vt* | (l.38) | set at the same time |
| cult *n* | (l.65) | group following the same patterns of behaviour (mostly used for religious groups) |
| mob *n* | (l.65) | group following the same patterns of behaviour (mostly used for disorderly crowds often involving violence) |
| brink *n* | (l.68) | edge |
| frown upon *v phr* | (l.88) | disapprove of |
| take precedence over *v phr* | (l.91) | be more important than |
| stove *n* | (l.118) | appliance for cooking or heating |

## 3 Text

While reading the text find the answers to the following questions:
a)  What two examples of 'time sickness' are given in the text?
b)  What causes the biological clocks of almost all living things to change?
c)  In southern Europe are people or schedules more important?

# ■ HOW TO TAKE YOUR TIME

D r Larry Dossey has two anti-
que clocks. 'One fast, the
other slow,' says Dr Dossey.
'They remind me that my life is not
5 ruled by clocks, that I can choose the
time I live by.'

How a person thinks about time
can kill him, according to Dossey, a
pioneer in the emerging science of
10 chronobiology, the study of how time
interacts with life. One of the most
common ills in our society, he says, is
'time sickness', a sense of time pressure and hurry that causes anxiety and
15 tension. These symptoms predispose
their victims to heart disease and
strokes, two of our most frequent
causes of death.

Dossey has discovered that these
20 and other stress-induced ills can often
be successfully treated by using simple techniques to change how a person thinks about time.

Dr Dossey became interested in
25 time and health when he noticed how
many patients insisted on having
watches with them in hospital, even
though they had no schedules to
keep. They were all time addicts,
30 taught since childhood to schedule
their lives by society's clock, and all
felt lost without the security of a
timepiece. Time seems to rule our
lives. Time is money, to be saved and
35 spent wisely, not wasted or lost.

Almost all living things in our
world carry their own biological
clocks synchronised with the rhythms
of nature. Crabs can sense when the
40 tide is about to change. The nocturnal
mouse wakes when night nears. The
squirrel knows when to prepare for its
long winter nap. These living clocks
are not accurate in any robot-like
45 mechanical sense. They adjust to
changes in the environment.

Light is the most powerful synchroniser in most living things. But in
humans there is another powerful
50 synchroniser: other people. Pioneer-
ing studies in West Germany reported
that when people were put together
in groups isolated from external time
cues of light, temperature and humid-
55 ity, their own complex internal
timekeeping rhythms became desyn-
chronised; then they resynchronised
in unison. Even body temperatures
started to rise and fall together, a
60 sign that subtle biochemical changes
in each body were now happening
together. The experiments may have
discovered one of the mysterious
forces that reshape individuals into
members of a team, cult or mob.

The mind can alter rhythms of time
in various ways. People brought back
from the brink of death often recall
their entire lives flashing before them
in an instant. Those who have been in
a serious accident often report that,
as it occurred, everything happened
in slow motion; apparently this is a
survival tool built into the brain, an
ability to accelerate to several times
normal perceptual speed, thereby
'slowing down' the world and giving
the victim 'time' to think how to
avoid disaster.

Because the time our society keeps
has been taught to us since birth, we
think of it as something that everyone
everywhere must somehow share. But
cultures differ in how they perceive
time. In North America and the industrialised countries of northern
Europe life is tightly scheduled. To
keep someone waiting is frowned
upon. But in southern Europe and,
by extension, in the Hispanic countries of Latin America, people take
precedence over schedules — and in
making appointments a more flexible
starting time is assumed.

Each view of time has advantages
and disadvantages. But the costs can
be great. When our natural inner
rhythms are out of synchronisation
with clock time, stress results. Under
the tyranny of clock time, western
industrialised society now finds that
heart disease and related ills are leading causes of death. However, such
'time illnesses' can be treated and
prevented by changing the way we
think about time according to Dr
Dossey. He applies simple techniques
that you can also use to change and
master your own time:

1  Unlock your life.
Stop wearing a wristwatch. Time becomes much less a concern when we
break the habit of looking at clocks or
watches.

2  Set your own inner sense of time.
To illustrate that time is relative, Ein-
stein observed that to a person sitting
on a hot stove, two minutes could feel
like two hours; to the young man with
a pretty girl, two hours could seem
like two minutes.

3  Tap your body's power to change
time.
We all possess an inborn ability to

relax. Most people can summon it up merely by dismissing intrusive thoughts and by controlling their breathing — for example, by thinking the word 'one' with each outgoing breath. Within several minutes this can produce deep calm.

4 Synchronise yourself with nature. Take time to watch a sunset, or a cloud cross the sky. Remember that there is a time far older than what humankind has created with clocks.

The cultural pattern we call time is learnt, and if we wish to live in harmony with nature we must learn to recognize that its time still shapes our 140 world and should not be ignored. We created the mechanical time by which our society clocks itself, and we have the freedom to choose whether we will be its slave or its master. 145

*(Reader's Digest © 1983; article by Lowell Ponte)*

# 4 Language study

### a) Vocabulary: power

The following words taken from the text all deal with power. Complete the word table.

| Person | System | Action |
|--------|--------|--------|
| master |        |        |
| slave  |        |        |
|        | tyranny |       |
| —      | power  |        |
|        |        | to lead |
| —      | force  |        |

### b) Useful words and phrases: expressions with 'time'

The following expressions all contain the word 'time'. Match the expression on the left with its meaning on the right.

1 to spend time

2 to waste time
3 to take one's time
4 to kill time

5 to play for time
6 to pass the time

a) to act in a manner that delays a decision or event
b) to do things at a moderate pace
c) to use time doing something
d) to fill up the time by doing something, however useless
e) to lose time
f) to make time pass quickly by doing something

### c) Language focus: manner and time

Look at the following ways in which these concepts are expressed in the text:
**1 Manner**
*how* time interacts with life. (1.10)
ie   the manner/way in which time interacts with life
*how* a person thinks about time ... (1.22)
*by* using simple techniques ... (1.21)
*by* changing the way we think about time ... (1.105)
*how* to avoid disaster. (1.78)
ie   the manner in which one can/ought to avoid disaster
**2 Time**
*when* he noticed ... (1.25)
*when* the tide is about to change ... (1.39)
*in* making appointments ... (1.92)
ie   when making appointments
*when* to prepare ... (1.42)
ie   when it must prepare

### d) Activity

Using the manner and time indicators given above, rewrite the following sentences so that they mean the same as the ones given: The first one has been done for you.

1  Instinct conditions the way animals behave.
   Instinct conditions how animals behave.

2  At birth some animals already know what methods are needed to catch or find food.

3  Others learn by repetition of their parents' actions.

4  Nature ensures that animals know when they must prepare for the reproduction cycle.

5  When nature provides the conditions for survival, it ensures the continuation of the species.
   _____, nature _____.

Now complete the following text by inserting one of the following words:
*how / by / when / in*

(1) _____ assessing the quality of twentieth century life, we need to balance certain advantages and disadvantages. The problem is (2) _____ to fix a value on those aids to living, and (3) _____ to admit that (4) _____ joining the rat-race to acquire them, the real quality of life suffers. However, in the absence of a fixed scale, we are unlikely to find out (5) _____ to improve our own lives or (6) _____ to stop looking for the key.

# 5  Transfer

## a)  Text

1  Complete the following 'time sickness' table. In the table '=' means 'consists of' and '⟶' means 'leads to':

```
                        1. _____
                              ⟶   { 3. _____ }    { 5. _____ }
Time sickness  =                  {            } → {            }
                              ⟶   { 4. _____ }    { 6. _____ }
                        2. _____
```

2  Now complete the following table about living things and humans, using the information from the text:

| Living things | | Humans |
|---|---|---|
| General synchronisation mechanism | Specific synchronisation mechanism | Desynchronisation mechanisms |
| 1 | 2 | Isolation from:<br>3<br>4<br>5 |

## b)  Discussion

Without a disciplined approach to time, it is doubtful that the industrialised civilisations could have developed.

# 6  Writing

**Write about one of these:**

a)  Write a letter to a friend explaining why you've decided to stop wearing a watch.

b)  Time is money.

# 1 Setting the scene

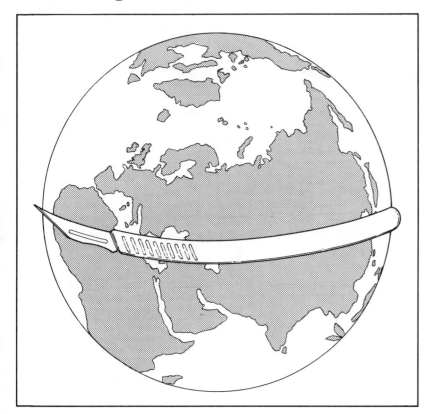

# 2 Vocabulary

| | | |
|---|---|---|
| hop *vi* | (1.4) | travel a short distance |
| taboo *n* | (1.8) | something forbidden for social or religious reasons |
| overalls *n pl* | (1.21) | special working clothes often worn over normal clothes |
| laser *n* | (1.33) | apparatus for producing a very powerful narrow beam of light |
| cataract *n* | (1.45) | growth on the eye |
| opaque *adj* | (1.46) | not allowing light to pass through |
| paralyse *vt* | (1.60) | cause loss of feeling |
| incision *n* | (1.67) | cut |
| transplant *n* | (1.91) | removal of an organ from one person and giving it to another |
| scarring *n* | (1.92) | mark left by wound |

# 3 Text

While reading the text find the answers to the following questions:
a) What are the three purposes of Project Orbis?
b) At the time of his Project Orbis operation, how many cataracts did Ghazy have?
c) Where did doctors in Alexandria use to obtain eyeballs?

160

# ■ A NEW SIGHT IN THE SKY

Thousands of people around the world owe their sight to Project Orbis, a medical team that hops from country to country performing operations, bringing the latest technology and teaching new skills. On this trip to Egypt, they also broke down an ancient taboo about life after death.

Built in 1959, the DC8 plane now travels the world as a flying eye hospital run by an international charity, Project Orbis. In Malta the project had just demonstrated the latest methods of eye surgery to doctors on the island. Now the Orbis mission was heading for Egypt.

It took just 84 minutes to change the plane into a working hospital. The pilot and co-pilot took off their uniforms and put on yellow overalls. Transformed into ground crew, they opened the belly of the aircraft, took out the cargo of medical supplies and lowered the heavy units which provide the ground power-supply.

A complete operating theatre and anaesthetic room was set up in the central portion of the plane. Instruments were unwrapped from foam packaging and put in place. In the galley at the front of the plane — the former first-class section — two laser operating microscopes were unpacked and the back of the plane was changed into a recovery area with three beds and a nursing station. Finally, the operating suite was cleaned and sterilised and the flying hospital was ready for use.

Abdelgabi Ghazy, a 60-year-old retired post-office worker, was one of those chosen for treatment out of the hundreds of hopeful patients. He had had cataracts in both eyes. The lens in the eye goes opaque in people suffering from cataract and must be removed. The one in his right eye had already been removed by a standard technique but he had difficulty in seeing well enough to walk round a room. He was selected to show the benefits of the most advanced type of cataract surgery on his left eye, which had not been operated on before.

Ghazy was made comfortable on a bed at the back of the plane. The anaesthetists injected a local anaesthetic into Ghazy's cheek and in the back of his eye. This paralysed the muscles in and around his eye so that he would not move or feel pain.

After removing the cataract Dr Stephen Slade then took an artificial plastic lens, about a quarter of an inch across and, grasping it with forceps, stuck it through the incision in front of the eye.

The next day Ghazy could see well enough to walk around without help. The artificial lens gave him a clear picture. It only has one disadvantage when it is compared with the human lens — it has a fixed focus. This is usually set at five to ten feet so that people can best see their immediate surroundings. But with the help of reading glasses, Ghazy could also read the finest available print. He now had 20/20 vision — the best.

'Allah be praised. I can now see perfectly. I am very happy. Thanks be to God,' said Ghazy.

Although some see Orbis as an outrageous gimmick, it works because of the teaching it does and the attention it gets from politicians in almost every country it visits. Part of that education involves changing cultural attitudes towards medical science, such as overcoming taboos about transplants. Scarring of the cornea, the transparent window of the eye, is, after cataract, the most common cause of blindness in Egypt and many other parts of the world. This kind of blindness can be completely cured by transplantation of a cornea taken from a dead person.

Since the times of the Pharoahs Egyptians have believed that a person must remain intact after death in order to proceed whole into the afterlife. Today modern Egyptians, whether Muslim or Coptic Christian, still believe that the body should be buried whole.

Most of the corneas transplanted in Alexandria used to be obtained by stealing eyeballs from corpses in the hospital mortuary. The surgeons who stole them used to replace them with glass eyes so that no one would notice.

'I find the idea of donating my eyes repulsive, although I have often taken them from other people,' said Professor Korra. 'The idea that my eyeballs will be thrown away after the corneas have been removed repels me.' But then Korra reasoned that it was possible to remove just the cornea from a dead body and leave most of the eyeball behind — enough for him to agree to sign a document and announce in public that he would give his corneas in this way and hope that others in Egypt would do the same.

*(From **Sunday Times Magazine**, 25 May 1986; article by Oliver Gillie)*

# 4 Language study

## a) Vocabulary: science and medicine

Below are some vocabulary items from the fields of science and medicine. Complete the word table:

| Noun | Adjective |
|---|---|
| surgery | |
| | medical |
| | operating |
| incision | |
| science | |
| technology | |
| method | |
| vision | |
| | blind |

## b) Useful words and phrases: verb + particle phrases

Below are some verb + particle phrases taken from the text. The particle in each case has been omitted. Complete the phrases:

1  to operate _____ a patient
2  to break _____ a taboo
3  to head _____ Egypt
4  to take _____ one's uniform
5  to set _____ the equipment
6  to take _____ the equipment
7  to compare _____ a human eye
8  to throw _____ the eyeballs

## c) Language focus: passives

The text contains a number of examples of passive constructions. They are listed below by tense.

1  Present simple
— when it is compared with the human lens
2  Past simple
— instruments were unpacked
3  Present perfect simple
— after the corneas have been removed
4  Past perfect
— the one in his right eye had already been removed
5  Future with 'will'
— the idea that my eyeballs will be thrown away
6  Modal + passive infinitive
— this kind of blindness can be completely cured

## d) Activity

Rewrite the following sentences in the passive. Mention the agent only where necessary. The first one is done for you.

1  Now we perform this type of operation every day.
   Now this type of operation is performed every day. _____

2  We started this project five years ago.
   _____.

3   During this period our team has made significant progress in this field of medical science.

_____

4   Up to about five years ago no one had investigated this area.

_____

5   Now we see that we can achieve results.

_____

6   So we will put pressure on world organisations to provide finance.

_____

7   At present major health organisations are making some progress in fighting endemic diseases.

_____

8   But we would have seen much better results if we had controlled the projects more effectively.

_____

9   In hindsight we needn't have spent so much on campaigns in Europe.

_____

10  However I am sure that these projects are going to convince the world of the need for more finance.

_____

# 5   Transfer

## a)   Text
Complete the following summary table about Project Orbis and their visit to Egypt:

| | | |
|---|---|---|
| Professional specialisation of Project Orbis | | _____ |
| Divisions of plane for medical purposes | 1 | _____ |
| | 2 | _____ |
| Disadvantage of artificial lens | | _____ |
| Two most common causes of blindness in Egypt | 1 | _____ |
| | 2 | _____ |

## b)   Discussion
We should donate all our organs to medical science for the future benefit of mankind.

# 6   Writing

**Write about one of these:**
a)   Describe the medical service and facilities in your area or country.
b)   Does medical science hold the key to all our problems?

# 1  Setting the scene

# 2  Vocabulary

| | |
|---|---|
| bizarre /bɪˈzɑː/ | very strange |
| clench /klentʃ/ | hold tightly |
| jaw /dʒɔː/ | part of face in which teeth are set |
| lung /lʌŋ/ | breathing organ in the chest |
| friction /ˈfrɪkʃən/ | two objects rubbing together (and producing noise) |
| drill /drɪl/ | tool for making holes |
| yell /jel/ | shout very loudly |
| ear-plugs /ˈɪə plʌgz/ | material put in the ears to keep out noise |

# 3  Tape

In this unit you will hear a discussion about snoring. Mary is complaining about her husband to June, who happens to be a doctor, but not a specialist in the problem under discussion.
While you are listening find the answers to the following questions.
a)   How does June, the doctor, describe snoring?
b)   Which two parts of the body cause snoring?
c)   Do you think June considers snoring to be a serious medical condition?

# 4  Language study

**a)  Vocabulary: organs of speech**
Below are some of the parts of the body mentioned on the tape.

164

Label the diagram with the items listed below:

lower teeth
tongue
vocal cords
nasal cavity
windpipe
hard palate
soft palate
uvula

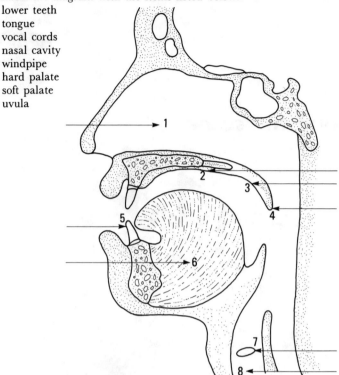

### b)   Useful words and expressions: annoyance and reassurance

The following expressions indicate annoyance or reassurance.

Write an 'A' to indicate annoyance or an 'R' to indicate reassurance:

I'm at the end of my tether.   _____

Don't let it get you down.   _____

I can't put up with . . . .   _____

I can't take . . . .   _____

Don't worry about . . . .   _____

Set your mind at rest.   _____

### c)   Language focus: suggestions

The two women use a number of expressions to make suggestions. These can be classified as follows:

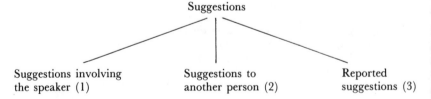

Suggestions

Suggestions involving the speaker (1)   |   Suggestions to another person (2)   |   Reported suggestions (3)

Now look at the following examples:

1   Why don't we talk about it?
    Let's not discuss this any more.
    I suggest we try another method.

2   You should turn him over.
    You could always try going to bed first.
    Why don't you try ear-plugs?
    How about giving me some useful advice?
    You'd better just put up with it.

3   Our local doctor recommended some rather bizarre practices.
    He suggested the following exercises.
    He recommended that my husband take . . . (note the subjunctive)
    He advised my husband to press . . .

Notice the following constructions:
— suggest (that) + subordinate clause
— suggest + something
— advise someone + 'to' + infinitive
— recommend (that) + subordinate clause
— recommend someone + 'to' + infinitive
— recommend something

### d) Activity

Transform the following sentences into the suggestion type (1, 2 or 3) indicated in brackets, using the words given The first one has been done for you.
1 You should stay in bed. (3)
  The doctor suggested that I stay in bed.
2 He recommends that I take a rest. (2)
  Why _____?
3 Let's not discuss this now. (1)
  I suggest _____.
4 He advised me to try a different medicine. (2)
  You could _____.
5 He recommends us to take as much fresh air as possible. (1)
  Let's _____.
6 How about your husband sleeping in a separate room? (3)
  He suggested _____.

Now look at the following suggestions, and indicate if the sentence is grammatically correct or not. If you think the sentence is wrong, then correct it.
1 The doctor suggested me to continue with the treatment.
2 He advised that I take more exercise.
3 He recommended to jog.
4 He also suggested me swimming
5 Finally he recommended that my partner exercise with me.

## 5 Transfer

### a) Tape

Below are the suggestions made by Mary, June and the local doctor. Listen to the tape again, and indicate in the table who made the suggestion by putting a tick (√) in the appropriate column.

| Suggestion | Mary | June | Doctor |
|---|---|---|---|
| going to bed first | | | |
| sleeping in separate rooms | | | |
| wearing ear-plugs | | | |
| clenching a pencil between his teeth | | | |
| yelling 'shut up' | | | |

### b) Discussion

Snoring partners can destroy relationships.

## 6 Writing

**Write about one of these:**
a) Write a letter to a doctor asking for advice about a medical problem you have.
b) Describe an illness you have suffered from, and include any advice you were given by your doctor or friends for a speedy recovery.

166

# MODULE 12
## HEALTH AND MEDICINE D

## 1   Setting the scene

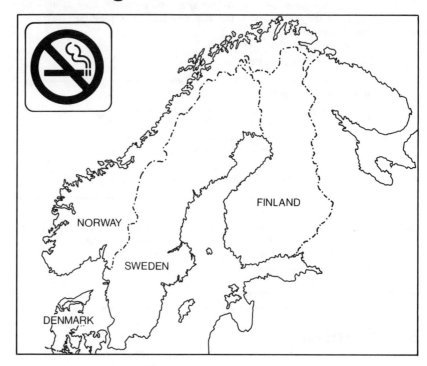

## 2   Vocabulary

| | | |
|---|---|---|
| legislate /ˈledʒɪsleɪt/ | make laws |
| overwhelming /əuvəˈwelmɪŋ/ | very much |
| abuse /əˈbju:s/ | wrong use |
| conclusive /kənˈklu:sɪv/ | certain |
| source /sɔ:s/ | place from which something comes |
| poster /ˈpəustə/ | large notice in a public place |
| expressly /eksˈpreslɪ/ | clearly |
| store /stɔ:/ | large shop |
| attainable /əˈteɪnəbəl/ | something that can be achieved |

## 3   Tape

This unit deals with the efforts by certain Scandinavian countries to ban smoking.
The speakers are a British visitor, George, and a Scandinavian, Erik.
While you are listening find the answers to the following questions:
a)   When, according to Erik, the Scandinavian, were the dangers of smoking identified?
b)   Which country is most lenient towards smokers and smoking?
c)   In what circumstances is a fifteen-year-old likely to become a smoker?

## 4   Language study

**a)   Vocabulary and pronunciation: language of legislation**
Below are some vocabulary items from the conversation. First underline the syllable that carries the main word stress. Then complete the word table:

| Verb | Noun |
|------|------|
| legislate | |
| act | |
| | opposition |
| permit | |
| limit | |
| | prohibition |
| ban | |

**b) Useful words and phrases**

Complete the following expressions taken from the text so that the verb phrase has the same meaning as the verb given on the right.

1  to _____ a step/steps    to act
2  to _____ a chance        to have a chance
3  to _____ suit            to take the same action as others
4  to _____ up a habit      to start
5  to _____ someone a hand  to help

**c) Language focus: volition**

The notion of volition can be divided into the following categories (1–4). The exponents of these categories are given in the appropriate column.

| | | Involving the speaker | Involving another person |
|---|---|---|---|
| 1 | willingness | will<br>to be willing to<br>to be prepared to<br>to be ready to<br>willingly<br>readily | to be willing for him to<br>to be prepared for him to<br>to be ready for him to |
| 2 | wish | to wish<br><br>to want<br><br>would like | to wish someone would + infinitive<br>to want someone to + infinitive<br>would like someone to + infinitive |
| 3 | intention | to intend<br>to mean<br>to plan<br>to aim<br>to be going to | to intend him to + infinitive |
| 4 | insistence | to insist on + ing<br>to be determined to | to insist that<br>to be determined that |

**d) Activity**

Rewrite the following sentences using an appropriate verb of volition. The first one has been done for you.

1  The government have expressed their intention to stop drug abuse.
   The government intend/mean/plan/aim to stop drug abuse. _____

2 They have expressed the wish that other organisations should co-operate.

_____

3 Other organisations want to offer help.

_____

4 But they are insistent that they must get funds for a major campaign.

_____

5 The government have indicated their willingness to contribute.

_____

6 But they have expressed the wish that a government department should co-ordinate activities.

_____

7 The organisations, on the other hand, are insistent that they should remain independent of government control.

_____

8 According to information obtained by the organisations, drug users have no wish to be under government surveillance.

_____

9 'No interference,' they insist. (Change to indirect speech)

_____

10 'Help is acceptable,' a spokesman said. (Change to indirect speech)

_____

# 5 Transfer

### a) Tape
Complete the following cause and result table:

| Causes | Results |
|---|---|
| 1  Smoking |  |
| 2  | Governments prepared to take positive action |
| 3  88 per cent of all Finns wanted tobacco advertising to be banned |  |
| 4  Sweden's less restrictive laws |  |
| 5  . | Success of efforts to ban smoking |
| 6  | Small percentage of children who smoke |

### b) Discussion
Government legislation to ban smoking is an infringement of civil liberties.

# 6 Writing

### Write about one of these:
a) Write a letter to a friend advising him/her to give up smoking.
b) What steps would you take to ban or limit smoking if you were a member of the government?